A SACRAMENTAL PEOPLE

Surely goodness and kindness shall follow me
all the days of my life.
PSALM 22

Michael Drumm and Tom Gunning

A Sacramental People

Volume II: Healing and Vocation

the columba press

First published in 2000 by
the columba press
55A Spruce Avenue, Stillorgan Industrial Park
Blackrock, Co Dublin

Cover by Bill Bolger
Origination by The Columba Press
Printed in Ireland by Colour Books Ltd, Dublin
ISBN 1 85607 289 4

Contents

For Anna

Introduction

This is the second volume of *A Sacramental People*. In volume one we addressed the sacraments of initiation – baptism, confirmation and eucharist. This volume is devoted to the sacraments of healing and vocation – anointing the sick, reconciliation, marriage and holy orders. There is also a chapter on celebrating death.

The intention of these two volumes is to contribute to the pastoral renewal of the sacraments in the life of the church. Significant numbers of people still attend sacramental gatherings and, with a little imagination and creativity, these celebrations could be an important focus for renewal in the church. Drawing on the links that exist between ritual and sacrament it is possible to renew our celebrations in such a way that they act as thresholds which can nurture faith, reflection and an encounter with our Paschal identity.

This volume is divided into four parts. Part One deals with the very nature of ritual; Part Two discusses some issues raised with regard to the sacraments of healing and the celebration of death; Part Three analyses the two sacraments of vocation – marriage and holy orders, whilst Part Four provides various ideas and texts for use in the celebration of the sacraments.

The two volumes follow the same format. The first chapter in each book analyses the importance of ritual in human life. This gives a foundation for a renewed understanding of the sacraments. In the succeeding chapters the reader will find a contemporary theology for each of the sacraments. In conclusion, each volume provides ideas and texts which could be used in sacramental celebrations.

The books might be used in various ways. The first chapter in each volume could form the basis of reflection on the very nature of sacrament and ritual for a discussion group. Similarly the theology of a sacrament could be analysed on the basis of the relevant chapter. Some might just read one chapter dealing with a particular sacrament which concerns them personally or which they could never really understand. Others might use the actual texts for sacramental celebrations that come towards the end of each volume. In other words, the intention is that these books be 'pastoral' in the best sense of the word – that they present a contemporary, accessible theology for each of the sacraments, that the individual reader can dip into them as he/she desires, and that they provide ideas and texts for the renewal of sacramental celebrations.

Part I

CHAPTER ONE

The Importance of Ritual

In the first chapter of volume one of *A Sacramental People* we analysed some principles that are significant in the celebration of the sacraments. In this, the first chapter of volume two, we intend to amplify and develop some of these principles. In doing so we invite the reader to reflect on the importance of ritual behaviour in our lives and we contextualise the sacramental life of the church in this broader framework. The diagram on p. 14 draws together in one image the various strands of the arguments put forward in this chapter.

The edge and the centre

One day every year a farmer asks to meet his neighbour to mend a wall that separates their farms. So the story goes in Robert Frost's poem 'Mending Wall'. The farmer wonders why they should really bother as his land is all pine and the other's is apple orchard. Yet the terse reply is that 'good fences make good neighbours'. Since nomads first settled down to domesticate a piece of land we have been driven to define what is ours, to erect fences, to establish beyond doubt our boundaries. Establishing boundaries identifies the limits of our experience, our knowledge and our ownership. We can control and structure that which is inside the boundary and so identifying the edge determines the centre, that which is structured, protected and ordered. It is here that we must live. At the centre, in the house or workplace, amongst family, colleagues and friends one finds comfort and security. It is the familiar. For some it is pensioned, mortgaged, insured life. In archaic societies too it was at the centre that structure and order was found. In the initiation ceremonies of the Kwakiutl of North America the novice is brought back to the ceremonial house after the ordeals of the forest. The novice then cries: 'I am at the centre of the world.' Within these ceremonies of initiation there is a sense of accomplishment and ending, a sense that in returning from the edge to the centre a goal has been achieved.

Given that the centre of things is so important, an interesting phenomenon of human life is our preoccupation with the edge. At the weekend people leave the city and go to the country, the mountain or the seashore to unwind and relax. Some even cycle off mountain ledges with parachutes, ascend precarious cliff faces and go to endless efforts to put their lives at risk. We long for vacation time when we can leave everything behind. Yet what is so seductive about the edge given that it is at the centre that we find order and familiarity? Is it that the centre cannot hold and so periodically we need to visit the very edges or limits of experience? What can be found at boundaries that cannot be found at the centre? Frost's poem can tell us something about what happens at boundaries. It would appear that the only chance for these two farmers to meet is in the crumbling of the wall. Yet the irony is that it is only in the destruction of the wall that they meet and talk and so it is a moment of creativity. The small crisis that befalls them every year actually maintains their relationship. Likewise those who climb rock faces, or set out on the ocean in crafts better suited to small lakes, create their own crises. Paradoxically these experiences become regenerative and creative. For many they provide a spiritual experience which cannot be found within structured religion. Experiences at the edge can be transformative. When one reaches the edges of one's identity and then goes beyond, nothing is ever the same again. It is as if one has gone through a threshold.

Sometimes the allure of the edge can be fashioned from a deeper need. The preoccupation with leaving the known and venturing to the boundaries of foreign territory has echoes of an heroic quest. Forcing one's identity, embracing ordeal and crossing thresholds is an initiation of types. From present day Play Stations to ancestral myths, we are completely seduced by tales of leaving the ordinary and the familiar to seek boundary experiences of daring and triumph. There has been and always will be a dynamic, be it in story, drama, journey or lived experience, of leaving the familiar and moving to the unknown and eventually of leaving the unknown and moving back to the familiar. It is impossible to go from womb to tomb, from infancy to old age, without crossing thresholds. To experience the complete ambit of what it is to live a human life demands that we initiate ourselves continuously into the different stages of life. To do this we must leave the familiar and journey to the edge, seek thresholds and venture across them.

Rites of Passage

Arnold Van Gennep coined the term 'rites of passage' in the early 1900s. His research was based on the rites which tribes and societies perform when they pass individually or collectively from one place, state, social position or age to another. He said that in archaic societies there were always new thresholds to cross: the thresholds of summer and winter, of a season or a year, of a month or a night; the thresholds of birth, adolescence, maturity and old age; the threshold of death and the afterlife. Just as the life of the planet must change and develop, so too the individual person must encounter different passages. One cannot remain an infant or a child forever; one must enter new identities, those of adult, mother, father and old age. Life brings us to various edges and we must learn how to cross them.

Concerning these transitions, primitive people gleaned a particular insight from lunar symbolism. The moon waxes and wanes, is present and absent. Somehow after it waned it seemed capable of regenerating itself. Based on lunar transitions archaic societies accepted a principle of death and rebirth in the cosmos as cosmic systems periodically renewed themselves. Yet human life too had times of transition. Just as the moon can wax and wane and regenerate itself, there is a central principle of regeneration and transformation within the biological, psychological and spiritual aspects of human growth.

'Rites of passage' is the term we use to describe the rituals that various societies and institutions have developed to mark these important transitions in human life. Though the ritual behaviour of different groups varies enormously, they have one interesting characteristic in common – they share the symbolism of the edge or the threshold as a metaphor for what is happening to the individual and the group. Ritual behaviour in general tends to mirror this movement away from the centre and familiarity towards a threshold or edge experience. The experience of a threshold moment differs greatly from culture to culture and from one person's life to another. The threshold moment can be chosen and entered into voluntarily or it may be imposed and entered involuntarily, and so there is a distinction between the different layers of experience within ritual. Irrespective of these distinctions, what emerges is that all of life is in some way, voluntarily or involuntarily, bound up with the experience of visiting the edge and returning to the centre. As we begin to examine the different layers within the process of ritual behaviour, the reader will find them figuratively displayed on p. 14. We have deliberately chosen the image of concentric circles. In the smallest circle we find ourselves at the centre of life and in the outer circles we outline the many edges and thresholds that we choose to visit or that are forced upon us.

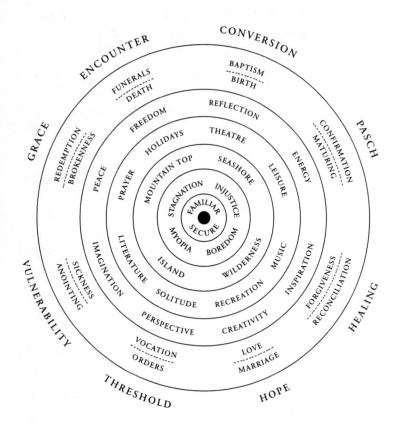

Landscapes and seascapes

The most straightforward way to leave the familiar is to journey to the mountaintop, the forest, the seashore or the glen.
Such thresholds removed from the centre, with its deadening
structures and familiarity, are places of perspective and renewal.
If we never leave the centre of life, the place where we live and
work, eat and sleep, there is a real danger of boredom and
stagnation. Worse, we can begin to live in a myopic world
with little sense of the injustice of so many structures. Human
beings need to encounter different perspectives which might
entice them away from worship of the false gods of security
and familiarity.

The mountain, the seashore, the uninhabited island, the wilderness of forest and desert, have played a critical role in the history of all religions and the development of various spiritualities. In the life of the human spirit, crucial moments occur away from home. Moses was told to go to Horeb, Jonah to Ninevah and Jacob to Haran. There is a geographical departure in all these stories. The call to the lakeshore or the seashore, the island or the brook, may not be a prophetic calling as those above, but it does bring fresh awareness and perspective because this is exactly what happens at thresholds. If one were even to stand in the threshold of a room it becomes apparent that there is a view of two spaces instead of one, that it is only at the threshold that one can enter or depart, that it is only here that one has a choice. There are possibilities and perspectives that can only occur at thresholds which cannot happen at the centre.

Creation is not opaque but a cipher for numinous and deep realities. To leave the urban sprawl and its stress, and taste the silence or breathtaking beauty of the natural world is not necessarily about being 'eco-friendly' or 'new agey'. There should be no cause for embarrassment in being seduced or inspired by the stuff of nature for it is God's creation. Much can be deciphered from the sea, the wind and the earth for since time began all of creation, as St Paul tells us, has been groaning in one great act of giving birth and it too, like us, is waiting to be set free (see Rom 8:18-22).

Thus far we have analysed the simplest form of ritual behaviour under the heading of landscapes and seascapes. We have noted that certain places are important in the history of religious rituals. But certain times are similarly significant – dawn and dusk, the equinox and the solstice, night and darkness. So too some forms of human behaviour can open the door to a heightened awareness – fasting and silence, touching and tasting, posture and odours. What all of these have in common is the capacity to bring us to a different threshold where we can see things in another way.

Dramas and journeys

There are endless roles to play in life: mother, father, teacher, priest, businessman, businesswoman. Each day in work people have to be attentive to their roles and wear the appropriate mask. Teachers have to be disciplinarians, business people should be shrewd, sales people must be sanguinely pleasant. It takes energy to play these roles, to maintain the tension between having to perform the duties of the workplace and doing what one would love to do. Yet these everyday dramas hold the centre together. It is how we support industry and employment, maintain essential services and earn a livelihood.

What is crucial to the maintenance of these roles is the ability periodically to remove oneself from the drama, to give the tensions a rest. It is vital to give time to the identity behind the mask, to wear different clothes, to laugh, to act spontaneously, to live life without a script. And life is an endless process of doing just that, of leaving the familiarised notion of self as employee or employer, child carer or parish administrator and journeying to the threshold. There are endless examples of these journeys: weekends away, holidays abroad, leisure activities, going to the theatre, bar or restaurant; reading the scriptures, personal meditation, going on retreat or sabbatical; reading, writing, hobbies and sport. All of these offer the possibility of leaving our masks aside for a while and encountering others, the planet, life and maybe even God, in a different way.

Whether one experiences landscapes or seascapes, dramas or journeys, one cannot but be seduced by the threshold. Look at what can happen there: freedom and possibility, change and regeneration, transformation and meaningful relationships. The journey to the threshold can be likened to revisiting the edges of Eden from whence we were once cast. Within the script and security of the familiar there can be a deep restlessness, a sense of paradise lost, that life can be better, that the centre can be more true, more meaningful. Without doubt, a paradise of sorts is found in some of these leisure activities.

The threshold is the place of meaningful encounter because those who meet there are truly themselves. Just like Frost's experience of mending his neighbour's wall, thresholds can become the location of creativity in life. There is no hidden agenda forced by the demands of productivity. Likewise, being alone and choosing to be away from the crowd can provide moments of genuine encounter with the deeper realities of life. In writing or meditation, solitude or prayer, one looks inside as into a well, going down for the good stuff, where the flame of clarity and truth can enlighten the darkness of silence and solitude.

In all of this there is one necessary and vital act, that of separation. One cannot experience what happens at the threshold unless one first separates from the familiar or one journeys in some way towards the edge. This can include a geographical movement, a change of setting, of clothes or of focus. Often in life this journey of separation is longed for, planned and saved for, yet there is a darker side to the threshold. Thus far we have considered the examples of times when we voluntarily move to the edge and away from what is common and banal. However, there are times in life when one is forced to the edge, when the movement is involuntary.

A fruitful darkness
There are experiences in life which are harsh and oftentimes unwelcome. To be forced away from the centre is more often than not a chaotic experience. And life does this to us at times. Bereavement is the outstanding example. When we loose

someone close, a familiar face and voice is missing from the
home, nothing can be the same again as familiarity has disappeared. Tragedy can strike in many guises and forms – financial, social, medical. A crisis can occur at any stage in life, particularly in times of transition or passage when we are forced
to leave something behind. Children must leave dependence
to become independent adults. All of us at some time have to
let go of the idea that we are still young, just as surely as we
must accept the idea that we have now become old. Life is a
process of letting go, of moving from one threshold to another.
Unwelcome as tragedy is, it needn't always be pure darkness.
Painful separations can often precede creative breakthroughs.
How many times have we heard of the family difficulty that
brought everyone together, or the personal crisis that brought
someone out of self-centredness and egotism to become more
caring and altruistic? How many times has crisis deepened
and made genuine our relationships, how many times has it
brought us closer to God? One can argue that it is only in crisis
and chaos, within the thresholds of sickness, loss and hurt,
that the most meaningful experiences emerge in life – forgiveness, healing, altruism, growth and transformation.

Let us view life as a process of being brought involuntarily
to different threshold moments. From the moment we are
born we are pushed from our mother's womb into a world of
love and loss, hope and despair, expectation and promise, life
and death. It is something we never requested, we are simply
landed into life. We grow to become children, yet as the years
progress it is demanded of us that we mature. We must separate ourselves from childhood ways and sacrifice dependency
and irresponsibility for commitment and duty. All through
life we will suffer some form of heartbreak, pain, loss and
hurt. Our relationships will experience rupture through forgetfulness, infidelity and selfishness. Hurt spawns bitterness
and regret, yet these realities can lead us towards thresholds of

forgiveness and reconciliation. Life pushes us in other directions as well. Nobody can design or plan love, it just happens and the happiness that it creates can sustain a lifetime of sacrifice and commitment. Others experience a desire to live life according to a different set of values. These are called to ordained ministry and/or religious life through which they craft their own interpretation of discipleship. Finally, sickness and death await the strongest and fittest of us all. All living things must grow feeble as the strength and vigour of life gives way to the unrelenting process of time. These are the thresholds that we must cross if we are to live truly human lives. Whether we like it or not we will be brought to these places.

Significantly, Christian tradition has made sacraments of these moments. Baptism initiates a person into the church and is often celebrated soon after birth, while confirmation, when it is celebrated in late childhood or early adolescence, marks a threshold on the road to maturity. The sacrament of reconciliation challenges us to live the reality of Christian forgiveness. Marriage and holy orders are the sacraments of commitment and vocation, whilst the sacrament of the sick gives strength to those who are ill or dying. It is the most basic insight of Christian belief that we live in a broken, fragile and sinful world. Redemption is to be found not by turning one's back on the sad difficulties of life but, like Christ himself, through embracing the realities that confront us.

Interestingly, no single threshold moment in life relates directly to the eucharist. But look at the diagram on p.14. In order to keep the centre renewed, creative, just and meaningful, it becomes the work of life to continually offer ourselves to the transformative power of thresholds, to separate, to find new perspectives. In the eucharist it is work like this that we bring to the altar. The key thresholds in life that we celebrate in many of the sacraments can often be extremely sacrificial in nature, be that birth or maturing, commitment or letting go.

Yet the gifts of bread and wine symbolise the offering and sacrifice that we make continuously throughout our lives. Just as we can be rent apart within the act of self-giving, so too the bread is broken, the grapes are crushed. We offer our own self-sacrifice, we offer the work of our human hands.

So far we have examined the ritual process and the rhythm of leaving the centre, being renewed and returning again. Sometimes the rhythm back and forth is voluntary, sometimes involuntary, but there is little doubt that significant change can take place: from childhood to maturity, bitterness to reconciliation, self-sufficiency to love, life to death. Yet taken at whatever level, one truth emerges and it is this: without ritual the centre cannot hold for there is no transition or change, no genuine relationships. Without ritual I go nowhere, I see nothing new and I do it alone.

At the Centre

If structure, order and the familiar define the centre, then within the church we have definite structures and an ordered and familiar way of going about the business of being a Christian people. Dioceses and parishes are organised in a very structured way and there is a particular order and familiarity to the liturgical year and our celebration of the sacraments. Our churches are often constructed with high steeples and thick pillars, suggesting the proximity and strength of our link with the divine. There is a comforting steadfastness and security about them. Within the above structures, faith and meaning, understanding and tradition can persevere and endure. All of this is as it should be and it is how all religions endure the persecutions of time. This is the nature of the centre. But we need to be aware that the centre cannot hold unless it is periodically immersed in the experience of the threshold and the edge.

A church bereft of an experience of the threshold could become prone to stagnation and myopia. Accepted understandings or interpretations would not be revisited and so the church could be condemned as irrelevant by a new generation. But there is a spirit within the church which frowns upon such an understanding of things. There is something unsettling and restless at the heart of Christianity.

After his baptism, Jesus is sent into the wilderness by the Spirit. And of this same Spirit John tells us: 'The wind blows wherever it pleases; you hear its sound, but you cannot tell where it comes from or where it is going. That is how it is with all who are born of the Spirit' (Jn 3:4). This is not the Spirit of stagnation or conservatism, but the Spirit of the threshold, of critique and imagination, of change and possibility. Strangely, and in keeping with what we know of thresholds, it is also the Spirit of chaos. In the book of Genesis we read that at the moment of creation there was a formless void, there was darkness over the deep and God's Spirit hovered over the water (Gen 1:2). There was chaos, yet this is where God's Spirit was to be found and this is also true of human life. Creation is to be found in chaos, in the fruitful darkness of genesis.

The church community which is bold enough to visit the uncertainty of the edge may have to experience the darkness of disorientation and the confusion of losing established patterns of understanding and doing. But this group will open itself to the possibility of true community and closer relationships. It will experience possibility and change. It will be a freer community, capable of embracing self-critique. In short, it will be a community that can realign itself to discipleship and gospel values. It will be a community based on the Spirit of creation and transformation.

Two thousand years ago Jesus preached the dawning reign of God. His message was anti-fashion, unconventional and disturbing. The reign of God runs contrary to prevailing values and opinions, as attested to in the many parables of Jesus.

They seem designed to disrupt our cosy views. In his first letter to the Corinthians, St Paul tells us that God's foolishness is wiser than human wisdom, God's weakness stronger than human strength (1 Cor 1:25). That God sees things differently than we do seems woven into the very fabric of Judaism and Christianity. For those who follow God's word there is serious disruption. Moses was sent to Horeb, Jacob to Haran and Jesus to the wilderness. That God disturbs comfort and inertia are threads which run through the fabric of divine revelation throughout history. Jesus lived his life on the edge, at the threshold. Why? Because that is where the divine can be encountered and Jesus, being the fullness of divinity present in humanity, invites us into the very life of God. But this is a difficult path because we discover that true community is found in poverty and disruption, that discipleship will push us to the edge and that little that really matters is the way it appears to be. Life appears almost as a negative of itself, the shadows become light and the brightness is shaded. Carl Jung once remarked that if a friend were to inform him of great news of promotion or financial gain Jung would commiserate. However, if the friend told him that some crisis had befallen him Jung would suggest that they crack open champagne. That we can hope in darkness is almost like a beatitude.

When we speak of ritual we refer to that dynamic in life of leaving the familiar, the banal, to savour something nearer the edges of experience. Life will bring us to these places or we may choose to go there voluntarily. It is the task of the local church community to ensure, at least on certain occasions, that its sacramental celebrations are indeed encounters with life on the edge. To congregate to hear the unconventional wisdom of the gospels, to savour the rich symbolism of Catholicism and participate in the very life of God in the eucharist, have the potential to be threshold moments. When we gather to celebrate Christianity we contest and challenge the isolation and stifling privacy of modern life, because at the centre of urban or city life this type of activity is fast becoming unfashionable. Our purpose now is to examine ways in which we can strengthen and reinvigorate the sacramental life of a Christian community. The following pointers, which include the insights which we have just gleaned from our study of ritual, might give a renewed focus to the sacraments.

Word and Symbol

Everyday we use words and language to communicate ideas, feelings and information. Words serve us well at a particular level, yet they begin to flounder when we try to speak about deeper realities, stronger emotions or the numinous. Poetry and music have the ability to find a deeper echo in our minds and hearts. Eventually, however, language must give way to other forms of symbolic communication. When meaning is no longer held, or begins to lose its moorings in language, it is anchored again in symbol. And when meaning begins to lose its moorings in symbol, it is anchored again in the word. In death we can often find no words to comfort because language simply can't express grief, and so we embrace. In love, two lovers may talk forever but their truest feelings will find expression in a kiss or the exchange of rings. If one were to try really to explain the effects of love or death, words would flounder and so language takes on symbolic expression. Symbols are born from language and story.

Symbols loose their meaning if divorced from the story which originally gave them expression. Wedding rings mean little if the couple who wear them are no longer in love. In this instance, the only way for the rings to mean something again is for the couple to revisit and rediscover the story of what attracted them together in the first place. Here a symbol desperately needs to be reborn again out of the story which first gave it life. Whilst words seldom require symbolic expression, symbols always require an appreciation of the story which gave them their origin. If we are presented with a symbol which evokes no memory, feeling or experience, then it is meaningless because we can't relate it to a story.

When we apply the above insights to our celebration of the sacraments, our attention should focus on how closely we align our use of symbols to the story from whence they originated. It becomes a means of presenting them more effectively. So, for example, a community must question how effectively it presents water as a symbol. What is so special about bread and wine? Why did Jesus choose to share his presence with us in a meal? Why do we light candles? What is so significant about light and dark? When we answer these questions we unify word and symbol, story and expression. It is crucial to be aware of the fact that symbols allow us access to the deepest of life's realities, feelings and insights way beyond the realm of language. Therefore to stifle the use of our Christian symbols either through minimalism or indifference is to deny a community some of its most profound experiences.

Awakening a sense of the edge/threshold
in sacramental celebrations
If I want to move to the threshold of a room I must first leave it. To move from the familiarity of the centre towards the edge, one must encounter something which is strange or do something which is unfamiliar. This is the nature of separation because the strange or the inexplicable awakens reflection. Separation perplexes and creates questions. It awakens.

There are many ways of creating separation, whether in the context of the sacraments themselves or in the context of celebrating our faith. Perhaps the easiest way to create separation is by going somewhere unfamiliar. Mountains, rivers, lakes, seashores, forests, ruins, or wells, can all be places of reflection and renewal. Deserts and islands can be more unfamiliar and therefore more liminal locations. It has always been part of the heritage of any religion that there are sacred places where one can encounter the divine. The scriptures are full of such examples. Just as there are sacred places, there have always been sacred times. Our forebears were much more in tune with the movements of the sun and moon. The solstices and equinoxes were times set apart for special activities. The movement of the liturgical year through the different seasons is not arbitrary, and the linking of Easter with spring accentuates the value of the story of Passover. These are sacred times and they set us apart, making us particularly conscious of some aspect of our Christian story. We normally celebrate our sacraments in daylight or electric light. Yet imagine in darkness the sense of separation that could be evoked by simply gathering together in candlelight. So too, dawn and dusk are threshold moments that witness the unfolding of darkness and light. The symbolic value of light and dark is immense and can be easily woven into the rich tapestry of life with its sadness and joy, its hope and despair.

Separation can also be created through the senses. We interpret our world continuously through our senses and we can immediately detect an unfamiliar sight, sound, touch, taste or smell. The sacraments have always seduced our senses and the church has long known how effectively it can communicate its message in this way. Just look at taste. Water, wine, honey, milk, vinegar, all have a Christian symbolic value as do salt, lamb, bread, oil, and herbs. As church attendance declines it would appear that there is an increase in the purchase of scented oils and candles. Yet our sacraments could be replete with candles, and the fragrance of balsam and incense. Even outside of the Christian story, scents, oils and candles have deep symbolic value and people will always be drawn to them. Remember that all of creation is groaning, waiting to be set free and so we should use the things of the earth to celebrate our redemption.

We have visited the many layers of ritual in life. Without doubt, ritual is vital to the wellbeing of the individual and society. It is the source of change, critique and regeneration. We examined the different layers and types of threshold moments that we can encounter. Those nearest the centre of life are not so unfamiliar, like seascapes and journeys. We noticed however that the most transforming experiences in life were in ordeal, tragic moments of loss and crisis, or at the threshold moments that are celebrated in the sacraments. These experiences are furthest from the centre of life and their unfamiliarity disturbs greatly. An experience of tragedy or passage cuts so finely that its effects are always buried deep.

Conclusion

The centre of life is characterised by habit and familiarity. It is comfortable and secure but nothing significant happens here; habit is anathema to imagination and change. Unfortunately the sacraments can often be experienced more at the centre of life than at the edge. Many will say that Mass can become a mere habit or routine, that it is tedious and repetitive. Others will condemn baptism as being ineffectual, no more than a social custom. And yet nothing could be further from the truth. The sacraments do not point to the centre but instead they are doors opening out onto the edge of life. God is not encountered in a life enslaved to routine, but instead in the vulnerability of pain and loss and in the openness of a cry that comes from deep within. The reality is that grace and hope can only be encountered when we are pushed to the outer edges of life's experience.

The sacraments receive their life from the events of Easter and consequently they are defined by experiences which are truly Paschal. At Easter we witness a humanity that knows isolation, betrayal and brokenness. Yet in spite of incomprehensible suffering and loss, at the empty tomb we find hope and healing. In the upper room there is doubt and despair, yet ultimately transformation and conversion. Those who see their lives woven into the narrative of Pasch will also see their lives in the bread that is broken and the wine that is given. At times they will have been overcome by the waters of the Jordan and assuaged by the oils of gladness and by the presence of Christ. The story of a sacramental people is a story of a people brought to the edge and to places where they would rather not go. Yet these are the significant moments of life; this is the place of healing. This is Easter.

Part Two

Sacraments of Healing

In this part of the book we will study the two sacraments of healing – anointing the sick and reconciliation. At their most intense these sacraments can truly be encounters with life on the edge. However, they often fail to make such an impact on the lives of the participants and their communities. We also devote a chapter to the ultimate human experience which is the threshold of death.

CHAPTER TWO

Anointing the Sick

The ministry of Jesus

Almost two thousand years ago Jesus of Nazareth spoke of the reign of God as healing for the sick, hearing for the deaf, new sight for the blind, freedom for prisoners, good news for the poor. Before we can really appreciate the meaning of healing, hearing, new sight, freedom and good news we need to become aware of the realities of sickness, deafness, blindness, captivity and poverty. When we look honestly at ourselves we discover that we are the sick, the deaf, the blind, the captive, the poor, and not just in some abstract metaphorical sense but in the physical, psychological and spiritual realities of our lives. Only when we immerse ourselves in these human experiences can we discover who Jesus really was, for his ministry was all about lifting burdens. Whether the burdens were created by a scrupulously strict religious sensibility or blind obedience or political corruption or grinding poverty or sickness or lack of self-esteem or pride or prejudice, the result was the same: people were in need of healing. The meaning of the miracle stories in the gospels is not that Jesus was some sort of esoteric magician who could solve all of life's most inscrutable problems, but rather that he was one who brought healing and hope into the most abject human situations.

The world is full of evil. Unless one lives a completely blinkered egocentric existence, the pain of human experience is all too obvious to see. In facing this reality we can turn our backs in despair or throw our hands in the air at the futility of human life. But the call of Christian discipleship demands otherwise. It demands that we always seek to lift the burden. Whether this means helping people to stand up and walk on their own, or exorcising their fear of the unknown, or exploding their minds through education, or feeding them when they are too weak to feed themselves, or opening their eyes to the reality of life, or challenging them to let go of hurts and prejudice, or liberating those who are unjustly oppressed, or introducing them to ever greater horizons of transcendence and beauty, or unsealing their ears to hear the divine echo in their hearts, or unleashing their hope for the future, or sowing the seeds of eternal life, the healing ministry of Jesus is continued as 'the blind see again, the lame walk, lepers are cleansed, and the deaf hear, the dead are raised to life, the good news is proclaimed to the poor' (Lk 7:22). Once a person receives the gift of healing then the possibility arises of moving on without the crutch or the grudge or the closed mind, whilst the future is no longer dictated by forces outside the individual but becomes an invitation to personal fulfilment.

Of all the questions raised by the existence of evil and suffering in our world, none is greater than this - why do the innocent suffer? This is the great question posed to all religious belief. Nothing so subverts our faith in humanity, in God, in the future. Nobody can explain life's most terrible tragedies. In the tradition of the Jewish prophets, of Job and of Jesus himself, we are asked to do our best to alleviate suffering, not to acquiesce in unjust structures which condemn people to endless pain, to hope against hope and, in the end, to surrender to a mystery greater than ourselves. We must not speak a pathetic message of joy and luck to a sad and broken world. Rather we must face the difficulties with whatever grace and dignity we can muster. Christian tradition tells us that suffering can be redemptive. It is hard to really believe this. Maybe the only way to discover what it could mean is to reflect on the reality of healing in our lives.

Healing

It is unquestionably true to say that the most important dimension of Christian discipleship is healing. The church exists not primarily to get bigger or more efficient in its work but to bring healing and hope into a broken world. All members of the church are asked to participate in this task of helping those who are blinded by prejudice or lame through addiction or deaf to others or dumb in bereavement or crippled by illness or imprisoned by history. The list of burdens goes on and on. In Jesus' ministry healing came through the spoken word and the laying on of hands. The human word of kindness, compassion and justice can indeed heal but words can also wreak havoc in their bitterness, apathy and prejudice. The word of healing will often be a word of honesty where we face up to the reality of human situations. Sometimes it will be a word of forgiveness which sets people free to move onwards. On other occasions it will be a word of comfort, often spoken in tears and heartbreak. But this word is always worth speaking, even when we might feel that it is useless or empty, as it is clear from the ministry of Jesus that the word can heal. Jesus also laid his hands on those who suffered. We should not underestimate the significance of human touch. At times it speaks more loudly than words and can give affirmation and strength to those who are in need. To be a source of healing, the word and the laying of hands demand faith. Obviously from a purely human point of view they can appear empty and meaningless. But when given and received in faith they can be a source of healing. One should note here that we are talking about healing rather than cure. Many people have been cured who were never healed and many who were healed were never cured.

Christians should interpret suffering and human limitation in the light of the death and resurrection of Christ. We need to look again at the meaning of sickness, addictions, psychiatric breakdowns, death, bereavement. From a Christian perspective one cannot just view these realities as disasters, but rather as part of the paschal mystery of Christ in which we all share. As we described in Chapter One, these are truly thresholds in life which we would prefer to avoid but which inevitably come our way. Even though we could never welcome these experiences, our Christian faith asks us truly to face up to them, for only by crossing these thresholds can we move on. Christianity does not provide escape hatches from life's problems but it demands that we encounter the true meaning of redemption at the very edges of our experience. This goes very much against the dominant cultural values of western societies today where human limitation in all its forms – sickness, disability, addiction, death – is frowned upon and ignored, hoping that it will go away. But Christians should take a counter-cultural approach in the embrace of human limitation and failure as the key to understanding who we are and what our destiny is.

The sacrament of anointing the sick

No sacrament is more misunderstood than this one. In large part this is due to its complex history. The use of oil for comforting and healing the sick was common in Middle-Eastern cultures. This theme is taken up in a famous passage in the Letter of James: 'If one of you is ill, he should send for the elders of the church, and they must anoint him with oil in the name of the Lord and pray over him. The prayer of faith will save the sick man and the Lord will raise him up again; and if he has committed any sins, he will be forgiven' (Jas 5:14-15). Note that this text refers to sick people rather than to those who are dying. In the early centuries of the church there is some evidence of sick people being anointed. This was intended to strengthen them in their physical or psychological illness rather than having some invisible spiritual effect or anticipating their deaths. Towards the end of the first millennium, anointing the sick became associated with the sacrament of penance. The latter was normally postponed until near one's death and so anointing also became associated with death. Thus it came to be called 'extreme unction', the rite associated with the last unction or breath of life. As this understanding became dominant it was felt that one could only receive the sacrament in danger of death and questions were raised over whether it might only be received once. Between the Council of Trent and the Second Vatican Council there was a renewed emphasis on this being a sacrament for the sick as well as for the dying, but there is little doubt but that in the popular mind being anointed by a priest was associated with nearness to death.

Vatican II introduced important reforms with regard to this sacrament. Most notably it changed its name from 'extreme unction' or 'the last rites' to 'the anointing of the sick'. As with all the sacraments it emphasised the importance of faith, the word and the community. The proper context for the celebration of the sacrament is communal, it must always include a reflection on the word of God and it should affirm and nourish faith. Three forms of the rite are now commonplace. There is a ritual to be celebrated with those who are sick, a distinct rite for those who are dying and a third form where the sacrament is associated with penance and the giving of holy communion.

The problem with the reforms is that they have made little, if any, impact on the popular mind of ordinary Catholics. Anointing is still perceived to be associated with imminent death. Let's turn our attention to this issue first. There are three sacraments linked to the death of a Christian – penance, anointing and eucharist (called viaticum when received by someone close to death). The final sacrament is eucharist and not anointing. This point is all important. The most significant sacrament of all seven is the eucharist; participation in it is the fullest expression of Catholic faith and it draws believers into the heart of the mystery of the death and resurrection of Christ. The most important journey that any human being ever makes is that across the threshold of life into the mystery of death and it is only right, if the opportunity arises (as clearly it doesn't in sudden death), to associate this passage with the eucharist by partaking of the body of Christ. If this renewed theology is be communicated to people in general then we need to set the anointing of the sick in a broader context. This is a difficult task, as no sacrament was in more need of reform in the light of Vatican II because it had tended to be always celebrated in a one-to-one context (priest and the very ill person) and often in a very mechanistic manner (almost akin to a medical intervention) due to the urgency of the situation. If we are to change people's perception of the sacrament then pastors and others need to take heed of the following issues.

Care of the sick and the old

One of the main intentions of the renewed rites after Vatican II was to move us away from any mechanistic understanding of the sacraments. With regard to the anointing of the sick, this demands a change in our approach to the sacrament. Illness and old age are not disasters awaiting to befall us but they are part of our paschal destiny. Nor are they purely physical realities marking our human demise but, for Christians, they are part of our journey towards divine fulfilment. As such they must be integrated into the life of the local Christian community. Everything from depression and addiction to cancer and cardiac problems to terrible results of violence and car accidents, and much more besides, exist in our communities. We must foster a sense of the whole community being responsible for those of its members who suffer greatly. There is a real temptation for the sick and the old to withdraw into lonely isolation. The Christian community must reach out to bring healing into the brokenness of serious illness and old age. Earlier we noted that healing in the ministry of Jesus was linked to the word and the laying on of hands.

In the case of those who are being cared for at home, the community, or some subsection of it, should gather to speak this word and lay hands on the sick person. The ideal context for doing this is during a celebration of the eucharist. Such a gathering should not be postponed until the sick or elderly person is too ill or feeble to play any part. During the Mass a relative or friend might speak words of Christian consolation and hope. The priest should invite all to pray for healing as he anoints the person; he might invite those present to link hands or to hold their hands aloft as he lays hands on the sick person. Remember that all of this is done in faith. We should not perceive illness or old age as purely physical realities; they are much more. Christians pray for healing not only at a physical level but also at a psychological and spiritual depth that goes beyond what the eye can see. Celebrating the sacrament of the anointing of the sick in the presence of the community of family, friends and neighbours awakens all present to the reality of limitation and frailty in our lives. If the sacrament is postponed until near death it is unlikely that the community can be present, the sick person might not even be aware of what is happening and it will probably take place in hospital. Priests, or others who must decide, should not be over scrupulous in determining who should be anointed nor the number of times that an individual should partake in the sacrament.

Many parishes now provide occasions when the sick and elderly can come together to celebrate the eucharist and be anointed. One Sunday in the year might be set aside for the celebration of anointing within the usual Masses on that day.

A parishioner who has endured a serious illness might speak of his/her experience in the light of the gospel. Again this has the advantage of integrating the seriously ill and the elderly into the life of the community as a whole. It will also continue the process of alerting believers to the fact that our faith is centred on Easter; Christianity is not just a human philosophy that one should be good to one's neighbour - it is the revelation that life and death are inseparable and that only through death will new life be born.

Care of the dying

In the sacramental life of the church the pastoral care of the dying revolves around eucharist, reconciliation and anointing. We badly need to rediscover the ancient tradition of the church that the food for the final journey (viaticum) is the eucharist. This is the last sacrament. Many people close to death naturally desire to receive absolution and to be anointed. When a priest is called to minister to someone close to death his first concern should be to carry the eucharist to this person. The opportunity for absolution might or might not provide itself. In this context, anointing is the least significant of the three sacraments. Of course practicalities dictate what can actually be done.

Ideally viaticum should be received during a celebration of the eucharist. Commonly this will not be possible. The rite for reception outside Mass is as follows:

> Greeting
> Sprinkling with holy water
> Penitential rite
>
> Reading
> Homily
> Baptismal profession of faith
> Litany

Lord's prayer
Communion as viaticum
Silent prayer
Concluding prayer

Blessing
Sign of peace

The intention is that this rite be celebrated with family
and friends. There is a notable emphasis on the significance of
baptism at this time. During the celebration of baptism, even
that of a child, the church notes that the individual is born to
die. It is apt then that as death approaches all present recall
the meaning of baptism when we were immersed in the
paschal mystery of the death and resurrection of Christ.
Communion may be received under both kinds during this
ritual though the very ill person may only be able to receive
under the form of wine. The eucharist is administered to the
sick person with the following words proper to viaticum:
'May the Lord protect you and lead you to eternal life'. It is
very appropriate that the ritual closes with the sign of peace.
The participants should not be shy about using song and
music at a time like this, when these heightened forms of
human expression can speak louder than the spoken word. If
the very ill linger for some time having received viaticum then
communion should be brought to them regularly for the rest
of their time amongst us.

Particular issues raised in hospital ministry
Because of modern developments in medical science and the
exponential growth in healthcare provision, much pastoral
care of the sick and the dying is now hospital based. This
leads to difficulties particularly with regard to the provision of
the sacraments. One principle should be absolutely clear – the
ordinary context for the celebration of the sacraments is the

parish and this is as true of the anointing of the sick as it is for any of the other sacraments. The problem with celebrating the sacraments in the hospital context, particularly the rite of anointing, is that it can be subject to gross misinterpretation. It is easy for participants and onlookers alike to perceive the priest's action in this sacrament as something akin to a medical intervention. It is nothing of the sort. It is an act of communal worship on the part of Christian believers who intercede for healing in the life of those beset by illness and infirmity. It should never be perceived as an action on the spiritual plane attempting to achieve much the same results as medical action on the human level in terms of cure or the lessening of pain. There is no similarity between medical intervention and sacramental celebration; the former belongs to the realm of human science, the latter is based on faith and hope in God's word.

Those involved in the pastoral care of the sick in hospitals should take certain steps to foster a deeper understanding of the meaning of sacramental celebrations in their work. In some hospitals this might demand that they call into question certain policies and traditions which, to put it mildly, have little to do with a proper understanding of the sacraments. Such steps should include the following.

(a) The provision of a space, even if it is small, where the sacraments might be celebrated. Whilst the sacraments will commonly be provided at the bedside, there should be regular occasion to celebrate them in a context which gives more space and time to explore the full meaning of the action. Such oratories or churches might also provide a space for reflection and prayer in a busy hospital situation.

(b) Clear efforts to awaken everyone to the fact that the last sacrament of the church is viaticum. Given that many of those involved in hospital ministry are now non-ordained, this emphasis is particularly important. Only ordained priests and bishops can administer the anointing of the sick. If people perceive the latter to be the last sacrament of the church then a priest will have to be called even if he is not the member of a pastoral care team who has been ministering to the particular person. Emphasising viaticum as the last sacrament would take away this preoccupation with anointing close to the time of death.

(c) Stopping the abuse of anointing those who have already died. The sacraments are the sacraments of the living, not of the dead. When a person dies we commend him/her to God's care. Many priests feel that they should anoint corpses in order to console the bereaved. In doing so they are reinforcing the misinterpretation of the sacrament in the lives of the faithful. It suggests a mechanistic intervention which can somehow influence the salvation of the individual who has died. There are many things which might be done by a priest or another minister instead of this. The corpse could be blessed with holy water, all present might be invited to trace the sign of the cross on the one who has died (as happens in baptism) and the group should be led in prayers that are familiar and comforting.

Conclusion
Through its rituals that deal with the sick, the infirm and the dying, the church makes clear that far from running away from these realities Christians want to lay hands and anoint, to speak the words of healing and touch the wounds of life. From the perspective of Christian belief the beautiful body is not that found on television commercials or magazine covers but rather it is the broken body in need of healing and strength. In John's gospel we read the famous story of Thomas who would not believe in the resurrection of Jesus unless he could put his hand and fingers into the wounds of his body. To have faith in the resurrection is to put one's hands into the wounds of life and still be able to believe and hope. In the

First Letter of Peter we read that 'through his wounds you have been healed'. It is only through becoming aware of our woundedness that we can ever know what healing really is.

CHAPTER THREE

Reconciliation

Nothing is more important in life than reconciliation. The most basic insight of Christian belief is that we live in a human world characterised by sin and failure. As a result relationships are ruptured, people say and do terrible things to one another, hatred and vengeance can consume our lives, jealousy and egoism can rule our hearts. In the midst of such sad failure Christian faith speaks of forgiveness and reconciliation. One should be careful in speaking of these realities, because words can be cheap but forgiveness and reconciliation are notoriously difficult.

Most adults can recall a time when they felt genuinely hurt by another person or an institution or a system. Presuming that they were truly injured, and that they didn't just want to take offence, what does it mean to say that they might forgive and be reconciled? At a human level, there are several arguments for attempting reconciliation. If one continues to bear the hurt then the offender dominates one's life and, as the victim, one's suffering endures. We often speak about forgiving and forgetting. If one can actually forget what happened so much the better because one can then move on. The problem with this is that most serious problems cannot simply be forgotten. In fact, such forgetfulness tends to be repression rather than reconciliation and so the same problem emerges later in life. One might try to clear the air through some honest dialogue. But this doesn't change the fact that the victim is the victim and the offender is the offender. When all else fails one can turn to the law courts to seek redress for the harm caused. But the law can be a blunt instrument and justice is not always done. From a human point of view, it is probably true to say that the best hope is that the problem will simply go away so that one can get on with one's life.

The Christian perspective on these realities is different. It is constructed on the premise that all of us are sinners, that none of us live lives without spot or stain, that all of us would be found guilty before a heavenly tribunal. This is why St Paul speaks about the law as condemning us. The religious law of the Jews (the torah) was meant to be liberating; through living a disciplined life in accord with the prescriptions of the law the believer would be freed from so much that is coarse and superficial in the world. But instead of being liberating the law became a burden and, measured against it, human beings were condemned by it. Maybe the best example of how something intended to be liberating can become oppressive is the command to keep the sabbath holy. What could be more liberating than the command to stop working, to take time off and look at the world in a different way, to be with loved ones in worshipping God and giving thanks? But the keeping of the sabbath itself became a great burden as endless minutiae had to be observed. That we could turn such a liberating command into an oppressive burden is sufficient proof that we need to be saved. Add to this our great difficulty in truly being reconciled and forgiving and it becomes clear that we are in serious need of help. That is why the early Christians said that Christ saved us from our sins. Paul said that we are justified by faith.

The language of justification sounds strange to modern ears but it is central to New Testament theology. What does the term mean? We often speak of the need to justify ourselves or our arguments. Paul's claim is that none of us can justify ourselves before God but that in justice we should be condemned for our failures. But the good news is that God has reconciled us in Christ, that the guilty have been acquitted, that sin has been forgiven. As a result we can be reconciled with one another for we know the depth of our own sinfulness. At a human level, we seek to justify ourselves, to stand our ground and to seek recompense when we are harmed. But for those who believe in Christ there is a new creation founded on the forgiving love of God revealed on the cross. The basic Christian message is the reconciliation of human persons with God through Jesus of Nazareth. The great biblical testimony to this is found in the Second Letter to the Corinthians.

> For anyone who is in Christ there is a new creation; the old creation has gone, and now the new one is here. It is all God's work. It was God who reconciled us to himself through Christ and gave us the work of handing on this reconciliation. In other words, God in Christ was reconciling the world to himself, not holding men's faults against them, and he has entrusted to us the news that they are reconciled. So we are ambassadors for Christ; it is as though God were appealing through us, and the appeal that we make in Christ's name is: be reconciled to God. For our sake God made the sinless one into sin, so that in him we might become the goodness of God. (2 Cor 5:17-21)

The early believers thought that after this act of reconciliation those who were part of the new creation would not sin again. The two great rituals of this new community were baptism and the breaking of bread. Through baptism believers were washed clean in the blood of the lamb and, in the eucharistic gathering, this new creation was celebrated and renewed. Right down to today the most important sacraments of reconciliation are baptism and eucharist. That is why at every celebration of baptism we acknowledge the need for the individual to be saved from sin and every eucharist begins with a penitential rite.

A distinct sacrament?

The first believers thought that, after baptism, they would never sin again. For if they did, that would surely nullify the meaning of their baptism. But believers did sin and sinned grievously. This posed serious questions about the very nature of Christian belief. Was baptism truly efficacious in taking sin away? If someone sinned seriously would that person have to be baptised again? Should the community expel such sinners given that their behaviour was scandalous to the faith of sincere believers? It was in coming to terms with these pastoral concerns that the church developed a distinct sacrament to deal with the reconciliation of those who had already been baptised.

The church decided early on that baptism could never be repeated. To do so would be to call into question the efficacy of what God had done in Christ. But the problem of what to do with the sinner remained. For lesser offences penitential exercises like fasting or almsgiving might suffice but, the serious sins of murder, apostasy and adultery demanded something more. This led the church to accept the idea of excommunication which meant (and still means today) that a member of the community is excluded from the eucharist. It does not mean, and never meant, that baptism has been revoked or nullified. Excommunication was a very public act and the sinner could only be readmitted to the eucharistic table after clear repentance and penance. This group of sinners was called 'the order of penitents'. The nature of reconciliation then in the early church was communal and public. The sin injured the life of the community and so the repentance and penance would have to be public. But that was to change.

The early Irish church had developed a distinct form of penance based on the monastic structure that dominated on the island. The system evolved from monks accusing themselves of even small transgressions and then being levied with the appropriate penance. This developed into a 'private' form of penance where the penitents confessed their sins to the priest who gave them the penance set out for the particular offence. This model of reconciliation was spread all over Europe by Irish missionaries in the seventh and eighth centuries. Over succeeding centuries this form of the sacrament became dominant. The confession of one's sin to a priest became the mark of the rite whilst the elements of conversion and penance began to fade. Thus the sacrament came to be known as 'confession'. In time the anonymity and secrecy of confession were emphasised and this led to the introduction of confessionals in churches in the sixteenth century. The Protestant Reformers of that same century rejected the sacrament of confession because they believed that it undermined the true meaning of salvation in Christ. Martin Luther used to attend the sacrament almost daily but he came to reject it as having more to do with human scrupulosity than faith in Christ. In the counter-reformation Catholic Church frequency of attendance at confession became a hallmark of pastoral practice, as the church sought to implement reforms which strengthened aspects of the tradition as a rejection of the Reformers' criticisms. Thus, in the two centuries before the Second Vatican Council, frequency of attendance at the sacrament of confession became a measure of one's identity with the church.

The reforms of Vatican II

The sacramental renewal that the council inaugurated has been particularly significant with regard to this sacrament. Modern scholarship had awakened a sense of the practice of the early church and, as ever, Vatican II wanted a renewed emphasis on the significance of the word and the community in the sacramental celebration. The popular name of the sacrament – confession – also came under scrutiny as it seemed to highlight only one aspect of the rite. These varied concerns led to important reforms. There would be a renewed emphasis on the word of God, conversion and the community. The words 'penance' and 'reconciliation' would replace 'confession' as better descriptions of the full meaning of the sacrament. And three forms for its celebration were introduced. We will analyse some of these issues in more detail.

The word of God

Given that the God of the scriptures is revealed as forgiving and merciful, it is important to incorporate the proclamation of God's word into every celebration of this sacrament. No matter what the context the minister, always a priest or a bishop, should read from the scriptures or quote them from memory or refer to a well known passage concerning forgiveness. This sets the context for what priest and penitent are going to say to one another. The sacrament is not a scrupulous analysis of human imperfections nor a heightened form of self-criticism nor an effort to overcome the debilitating aspects of one's personality, but rather it is an encounter with the forgiving love of God as revealed in Jesus Christ. The minister bears an onerous responsibility in this regard. Through his words and actions he must reveal something of the merciful love of God which through the ministry of Christ has begun to transform the world. The more the minister and penitent reflect on God's word the better will they appreciate the depth of human sinfulness and the breadth of divine love.

Conversion

The celebration of the sacrament should lead to an ever deeper understanding of the need for conversion in the lives of all Christians. The sacrament can easily fail to do this. People have often rattled off a list of rather basic human failings or even, in some cases, confessed sins which they never committed. Presumably the reason for this is that people don't know what to say and so turn to some ready formula or project some fault upon themselves that doesn't really exist. This clearly demonstrates the need for catechesis with regard to the meaning of conversion in the sacrament of reconciliation. Participants should be encouraged to reflect upon their lives in a very personal manner. They might ask: what's really worrying me? what keeps me going from day to day? does my Christian faith seriously impinge on my life? how do I treat my family and friends? do I ever think about those who suffer? The questions could go on but they are intended to lead the individual to speak honestly and in some depth about his/her life. Christian faith is not just a moral code against which we judge ourselves but it is a lifelong journey that invites us to discover ever new horizons of what it means to be human. On this journey there is no point of arrival, only the invitation to move ahead or the danger of slipping backwards. But one thing is for sure – rhyming off the same list of human failings over and over again is unlikely to lead one much further down the road of conversion. Similarly, the failure ever to speak honestly about one's Christian calling is unlikely to facilitate much growth and maturing.

The community

Traditionally this sacrament was understood in terms of privacy and secrecy. Whilst protecting the confidentiality implicit in the rite, the reforms of Vatican II intend to foster an awareness of the communal dimensions of reconciliation. Sin, though often deeply personal, is not private because its effects can reach far and wide. As sinners we need to become aware of the damage that our words, actions and omissions can do to others. This is one of the reasons why the sacrament exists. Our failures to live in accord with what we believe actually undermine the church as the body of Christ in the world. In the early church, as we have seen, this caused real difficulties and led the church to formulate a distinct rite for reconciling those who had been baptised but who lapsed into serious sin. The very origins of the sacrament lie in the need for the baptised individual to take his/her responsibilities seriously. That is why the church demands that we confess serious sin as the hurt that was done is not just a private matter between the sinner and God but has implications for the life of the Christian community. Because we live such private lives in today's western societies, this emphasis sounds strange. But retrieving the sacraments from the clutches of an all too private type of piety is an important pastoral goal.

The three forms of celebration

The present rite of penance and reconciliation allows for three different types of celebration. These are the rites for an individual penitent, a communal rite with individual confession and absolution, and the communal rite with general confession and absolution. The first of these is the traditional way of celebrating the sacrament and understood by the church to be the normal form of participation. This way of celebrating the sacrament can veer between the mechanistic, when priest and people seem to only go through the motions, and the truly meaningful, when the penitent and minister truly reflect on the nature of life's journey. Given that the sacrament can be so beneficial in the life of the individual Christian, priests should take care to foster a sense of worship and reflection. This can be done in many ways. The word of God should never be neglected. In Chapter Two we saw that the word can bring healing. Every celebration of the sacrament should begin with words from scripture. They prepare both penitent and minister to open their hearts to God's mercy. By his general demeanour the priest should encourage penitents to feel at ease and to express their concerns in their own words rather than in traditional formulae. He should

take care in giving penance; through creative suggestions
about reading, writing, walking, talking, he might open the
path to further self-reflection. Why not invite the penitent to
read a chapter from the Bible or another book that is particularly relevant to his/her circumstances or to write a note to
someone significant or to go for a walk in the countryside or
to talk to someone who has been neglected?

It must be accepted that people will vary in how frequently
they celebrate this sacrament. For some it has become a type
of devotion in which they participate regularly. It will naturally
prove difficult for the priest and penitent to foster a more reflective atmosphere in this context. For most Catholics it is a
rite that they have quietly abandoned or seldom frequent.
People feel alienated from the sacrament for various reasons:
some were forced as children or adolescents to participate in it
so regularly that it became meaningless; others had bad experiences with priests who were more akin to law officers than
ministers of the new covenant; still others see the confessional
as a symbol of darkness and fear which has little to do with
their faith; many simply cannot see the point in the whole ex-
ercise. To reach out to these members of the community it
should be made clear that they are only expected to participate in the sacrament once a year. They should be encouraged
to do so during the Lenten and Easter seasons. Similarly people should know that they can celebrate the sacrament outside the atmosphere of the confessional and that they should
feel free to approach any priest. But, most importantly of all,
Christians should be invited to think seriously about their
lives and to express their thoughts about themselves within
the confines of the sacrament. In an era of explosive growth in
all forms of psychotherapy we need to rediscover the spiritual
therapy of the sacrament of reconciliation. Bound as the minister is by the seal of the sacrament, it remains one of the truly
confidential contexts for self-disclosure and analysis.

The communal rite with individual confession and absolution has become common in many parishes. Its great strength is that it involves the broader community in the celebration of the sacrament. It also provides the opportunity for a more wholesome reflection on the word of God and a searching examination of conscience. Many pastors see a problem with this rite in that the confession of sin is understandably abbreviated as all penitents are asked to wait until individual confessions are complete so that the ritual can be closed in a communal fashion in keeping with the spirit of the gathering. But is this really a problem? Catholics are bound to confess mortal sins; lesser failings do not have to be confessed in the sacrament, not least because they are acknowledged and forgiven at the beginning of every Mass. Nothing has so changed our perception of the sacrament of reconciliation than developments in moral theology. Until Vatican II it was presumed that mortal sin was common; today we would be slow to suggest that any particular individual has committed such a sin. Therefore it is surely the case that large numbers of penitents attending the sacrament are not guilty of mortal sin and so there is no reason for them to go through a list of less serious faults. It is a good practice during these communal rites to suggest to the gathered community that those who wish to confess very serious sin might return to talk to a priest at a quieter time.

The third form of celebration of the sacrament is a communal rite with general confession and absolution. Those who receive such absolution must confess any serious sins to a priest as soon as possible. This rite can only be provided in cases of grave necessity. As always, such grave necessity includes danger of death. The other most obvious example is where a shortage of clergy would preclude people from celebrating the sacrament and therefore might also exclude them from the eucharist. The Vatican has made clear that such

necessity is not created by there being simply a large gathering
of people as at a pilgrimage centre or in a parish on Christmas
Day or Easter Sunday. The determination of what exactly
'grave necessity' means has naturally led to variations in the
provision of this form of the rite. It is the responsibility of the
diocesan bishop to determine if such necessity exists in a particular place and time. Therefore the practice can vary from
one diocese to another.

Conclusion

The numbers attending the sacrament of reconciliation regularly are in steep decline in many parts of the world. This
should not lead to undue pastoral anxiety. When one takes a
longer view of things, one sees that numbers attending various
sacraments have fluctuated greatly throughout history.
Maybe today we should change our pastoral goal so that our
energies are devoted to celebrating the sacrament with significant numbers of people once a year rather than trying to coax
some people to participate in the sacrament more regularly.
Finally, there remains the controversial issue of at what age
baptised persons should be admitted to the sacrament.
Currently the practice is to celebrate 'first confession' at seven
years of age. The reason for this is that seven was the age of
discretion in Roman law and once a baptised person reaches
this age, he/she is held to be in some way responsible. Modern
theories drawn from the social and human sciences question
whether a child of seven is indeed truly responsible, but it
takes a long time for such theories to impact on the traditions
of the church. It looks likely that we will continue with the
present age of entry to the sacrament for some time to come.
Be that as it may, the more important task remains of calling
all Christians to ever deeper conversion.

CHAPTER FOUR

Celebrating Death

It is impossible to remember our months in the womb; in fact it is difficult to recall our first couple of years alive. Our only access to those years is through the stories our parents tell us or an old faded photograph. That life which we once lived, though intrinsically part of who we are, bears little resemblance to the life which we now live. Physically, emotionally and intellectually we differ greatly from ourselves as infants. In effect, the infant that I once was has been transformed just as surely as the vigorous youth will one day change into an old man or woman. The journey from the womb to the tomb is a process of dying and letting go. It is a journey of learning and maturing into new experience and identity. In modern life the changes happen so slowly to us that they go unnoticed and so familiarity with our lives blunts the transformations that gradually do occur.

In contrast, those in primitive societies experienced rites of passage as they encountered the key stages of life and so had a sense of passing from one state to another, of dying to an old identity and giving birth to a new one. The most important passage was from childhood to adulthood and these rites initiated a person into the values and myths of a society and its spiritual realm. In order to learn how to come into the fullness of being, emotionally, socially and psychologically, a person first had to learn how to die. One could not become an adult unless the child first died. In initiation ceremonies, then, symbols of death saturated the neophyte's environment and they were filthy with the earth into which everything is rendered down. One can quite rightly say then that those in archaic societies first learned how to die through their rituals of initiation. Yet in Christianity the reality is no different. In baptism we are reborn into Christ and the church claims us as Christ's own with the sign of the cross. From the first few moments of Christian life we are marked by death. Those of us who are buried with Christ in the death of baptism are also reborn into everlasting life. And so it is in baptism that we first learn how to die. As St Paul puts it: 'When we were baptised in Christ Jesus we were baptised in his death; in other words, when we were baptised we went into the tomb with him and joined him in death, so that as Christ was raised from the dead by the Father's glory, we too might live a new life' (Rom 6:3-4). In the sacrament of confirmation we are reminded that we must be witnesses to Christ's suffering, death and resurrection and in the eucharist we are constantly called to participate in the death and self-sacrifice of Christ so as to share the new life that he brings.

Nobody can speak of what things will be like after we die except that we are baptised into an everlasting life with Christ and so that new identity which we were reborn into will have an eternal existence. However, there is a finality about death and an everlasting dying of the historical project that is one's life. The church teaches quite definitively that we are completely responsible for what we have done during our life span. What good we have done remains done yet what we have broken remains broken and unjust actions cannot be revisited.

Despite the fact that we cannot know what things will be like after death, it is only natural to want to imagine what sort of perspectives and experiences we might have. It is true that what lies beyond the threshold of eternity remains a mystery, but dying does not because the passages that we make in life require a type of dying. In adulthood the child must die, in marriage the single person must die, in old age the youth must die. In forgiveness, bitterness perishes and in self-sacrifice, selfishness is overcome. We know these places and have tasted the difficulty and darkness of letting go to maturity and altruism. The dying that we do throughout life is always a dying-for-another. If I mature or marry I do so for another. If I forgive, I do so for another and if I let go of individualism, I do so for another. In all of this there is a basic trust that this dying will bring good, that the transformation that will occur in this relationship will be fruitful and lead to intimacy. And this is true of life. Reconciliation and healing are wonderful realities but they are etched on the headstone of hatred and bitterness. Selflessness and self-sacrifice transform relationships and clothe us in the warmth of love, but first the ego must perish as it is stripped of what were once understood to be needful things. Life looked at in this manner does not teach us what lies beyond the threshold of death but it does tell us that the human lifelong process of dying brings the gift of maturity and more loving and genuine relationships. When we die for another we do so in trust and when we die in Christ we do so in the trust that we will live in him: 'If anyone believes in me, even though he dies he will live, and whoever lives and believes in me will never die' (Jn 11:25-26).

A Ritual Dying

Since our primitive forebears first observed the waxing and waning of the moon and the corresponding cycles of death and resurrection through the passages of a person's life, one truth has remained constant: death precedes new life and dying ushers in transformation. This is what the ritual process tells us about dying. Those in archaic societies knew this truth well, and so they didn't fear death as much as modern man and woman because they had learned through their rites of passage that life and death are inseparable. This sense of death as transformation was born and nourished through their rites of initiation, their rituals of dying and new life. Long after their rites of initiation were complete, primitives returned to their symbols of death and rebirth to experience the deeper dimensions of human existence and religious experience. Many today bemoan the disintegration of values and meaning that comes with modern life and so it is beneficial to look to those untouched by contemporary culture to learn what we have forgotten. Their closeness and reverence towards the symbols of death highlights our need to experience constantly the power of the Christian symbols of death and resurrection. We have become anaesthetised to the cross and the empty tomb through a familiarity which blunts the scandalous and wondrous reality of Easter. The Christian community should therefore spare no effort to re-imagine through song, story and dance the healing and redemptive symbols of Easter. We will only learn how to die as Christians by celebrating the ritual of death and new life which is the paschal mystery.

A Paschal Dying

Story has it that when Pope John XXIII was dying he said, 'My bags are packed, and I am waiting for her.' There is a sense in his words of fulfilment and promise. His words seem full of expectation and anticipation. His sentiments seem to contrast the wake-room and graveside scenes which many of us witness with anger and incomprehensibility. In the latter, death can be perceived as that which makes all of living and loving absurd. Why invest so much energy and intimacy in life when it can be wrenched away so easily, so futilely or with no word of warning? If death can make a nonsense out of the historical project of life and love, then one could easily loose respect for the gift of living. If life is an absurdity then it can be lived irresponsibly, dangerously and without regard. It can be perceived as a venture bereft of meaning, lacking in value

and worth. In order to search for meaning we would do well
to revisit the symbols of Easter, of death and resurrection.

In the incarnation God and humanity become one in the
person of Jesus Christ. In Jesus, God lived a human life and
lived it fully and died a human life and died it completely.
Jesus died, he did not slumber in the tomb for a short while.
For some his dying was seen as a disgrace and a scandal. It was
an absurdity, denying the conventional wisdom of what a
Messiah should be. His followers subsequently cowered in a
room entertaining doubt and denial. We were spared such
embarrassment, born as we were into a believing community
and even now the familiarity of the crucifix has numbed us to
the scandal that is our God bloodied and beaten like a lamb
led to the slaughter. On Calvary God experienced the darkest
aspects of being human and the utter absurdity of life. What
can be more inexplicable and meaningless than the innocent
butchery of the Son of God? And yet the cross has been transformed by Easter to become the symbol of our freedom and
redemption. Christ's sacrifice on the altar of Calvary can-
celled the effect of sin and made us one with God. It was the
moment of our atonement but it was also the moment when
Christ made sense of the absurdity of death. His dying was an
act of love through which he gave his life for others. It was
dying-for-another and his death identified the nature of his
personal historical project. Jesus came to save us from sin and
death and he did so by offering his own life. The historical
project of his life was accomplished at the moment of his
death. Calvary now defines Christ as our redeemer and saviour and so it no longer scandalises or confuses. Having
reached into the murkiest and lonesome parts of human existence, and even into death itself, Christ has transformed dying
into that which gives meaning to one's entire life: 'What shall
I say? Father, save me from this hour? But it was for this very
reason that I have come to this hour' (Jn 12:27).

The paschal symbols give us a new perspective on living and dying. It is as if with Easter we put on new spectacles and see the world anew. We live our lives and commit ourselves to relationships under the shadow of death. In this way, death actually defines the nature of how we live and how we relate to others. We live and love in the knowledge that one day it will all be gone. We live, create, imagine and love despite the eventual annihilation of this project and yet our lives are more worthy and selfless because of this. Dying becomes the ultimate self-sacrifice as we must leave the life into which we have invested so much. All our living then can be seen as paschal and the fulfilment and consummation of this life is in dying.

An Easter People

We emphasised in Chapter One that the most meaningful realities in life – grace, healing, forgiveness and genuine relationships – are experienced through brokenness, hurt, sickness and loss. There is a very definite dynamic here of dying and new life. The early Christian communities initially expected Christ to return and raise the dead within the course of their lives. Gradually, however, they came to understand that Christ was still truly present to them in the breaking of the bread and that his death and resurrection were realities to be experienced on this side of the grave. The reality of Christ's resurrection could be witnessed as these people, full of fear and doubt, were transformed into a Pentecostal community characterised by faith and celebration.

There is a temptation to wait for everything to be put right after death, to play a waiting game according to some promise that all injustice and disappointment will somehow be erased at the moment of dying. Yet, in effect, this is to avoid the responsibility that we are called to make salvation a reality now. Those alienated, impoverished and marginalised need salvation now whilst they are alive. Life and living has been redeemed by

Calvary and so our experience of being saved is not depend-
ant upon dying. A person will know they are saved when they
are taken from impoverishment or exclusion, loneliness or
hurt. We were called in baptism into the death and resurrection of Jesus Christ and it is only by dying with him that we
will live with him. But that dying starts today. In the eucharist
we are called to self-sacrifice, to continuously die to selfishness
so as to live for others, to know the needs of those gathered
around the table which is the altar of Christ's death. Like
those early Christian communities we must learn that resurrection happens in the authenticity of caring for others and
attending to another person. Like Christ, our lives will be accomplished when we die for others and, like Christ, we will
rise to new life from the tomb of self-emptying love: 'If we
have died with him, then we shall live with him. If we hold
firm, then we shall reign with him' (2 Tim 2:11-12). We cannot
and do not know the details of eternity, just as surely as we
cannot and do not understand what happens at the moment
of death. We stand, as it were, on the border crossing between
the lands of life and death yet we must turn back into the land
of the living for it is here that we must learn how to die.

Funeral Rites
Cultures vary enormously in their manner of disposing of the
dead. Even within Christianity one will find significantly different patterns of behaviour between one ethnic group and
another. This is to be welcomed, as no traditions are more ex-
pressive of a group's indigenous practices than funeral customs.
The rites of the church allow for such cultural adaptation and
pastors should foster an intermingling of Christian and native
traditions. However, the greater difficulty that we must face
today is a new one posed by modern Western societies.

There is a real denial of death in advanced western societies. In fact, the sense of denial is so great that it is one of the

factors that would lead one to question how advanced this civilisation really is. With the onslaught of massive conurbations all sense of kindred ties and community begin to unravel. The results are there for all to see. Whilst we live much more efficient lives compared to our forebears, allowing for extraordinary mobility, the danger is that our only measure of anything is in terms of its consumer value. In such societies, death gets pushed out into the realm of one more consumer item. We live in an era of professionalism based on the division of labour. There are experts in every field and we turn to them as our needs require. This has happened with regard to death as well. It is taken over by the 'professionals' in the funeral industry and the corpse is treated as something from which people almost need to be protected.

In this context, the Christian community should adopt a radical counter-cultural approach in embracing death as an integral part of human life. There are different ways in which this can be done, depending of course on the particular culture. Death pushes people to the outer edges of their experience. This is a place where common sense and ordinary language begin to falter. The rituals of the church are all important in beginning the process of grieving so priests and other ministers should take care to adapt the rites to the needs of the particular occasion. Hospital mortuaries and funeral homes, comfortable as they might be, are not the ideal setting for the gathering of a mournful Christian community; family homes and churches are just such settings. Families could be encouraged to bring the corpse of the deceased home. Nothing is more important in bereavement that coming to terms with the fact that the person has actually died. Also the family is truly serving the broader community by awakening everyone to the fact that death is at the heart of life. Significant numbers of people have never been present at an actual death and many have never seen or touched a corpse. These experiences, painfully difficult as they are, contribute to the formation of our true identity.

There are important issues raised in the funeral rites of children who die before baptism. Death that occurs so early in life is tortuous for parents to bear. Ritual is very significant at this time as our ordinary patterns of behaviour crumble in the face of such suffering. Before the baby is buried, if at all possible, the parents should participate in a ritual which includes the naming of their child. At the very least, this should be done at a later gathering of family and friends. It is very unfortunate if a child is not retrieved from the darkness of anonymity. Babies who are still-born or who die shortly after birth are human persons who, for whatever mysterious reasons, will never travel with us to the outer edges of human experience but whose death pushes us, against our wills, to those further thresholds. That is why we sometimes speak of them as angels, messengers who tell us something of who God is and what life is ultimately about. Such is the mystery of death and dying.

Part Three

The Sacraments of Vocation

Traditionally we used the term 'vocation' to refer to the call received by those who enter priestly or religious life, i.e. those who are ordained and/or live under religious vows. More recently the term has also been used with regard to Christian marriage. Ever since the calling of the first disciples on the shores of the sea of Galilee, the church has believed that its members are called to the service of the gospel in different ways. Some are called to be priests, others to live their lives under vows of chastity, poverty and obedience, while the majority put their lives at the service of God through the commitment and dedication demanded by married life. Traditionally a vocation was understood in a very simple way as if one could literally hear the voice of God. Today we place much more emphasis on the mediation of God's word to us through family and friends, prayer and personal reflection, the example and direction of others who have struggled with a particular vocation, and not least through our involvement in the Christian community and the effort to live in accord with the gospel. Through these varied realities, each individual Christian must seek to construct his/her own response to the gift of life and the gospel call to put one's life at the service of others.

There are three clear vocations in the Catholic Church – to married, priestly and religious life. Notice that they have much in common. All three demand that one's energy and efforts be put at the service of others; they involve the making

of a promise in the presence of others, as the Christian community celebrates and affirms publicly the vocation that the
particular individual embraces; they require a commitment
for life; they produce a completely changed reality in the lives
of those involved, as after the marriage or ordination or profession ceremony the person is recognised as having a radically
different identity in the Christian community. Nothing leads
to a greater misunderstanding of the meaning of Christian
vocation that mistaking it for a job or type of employment.
One often hears people saying that certain forms of employment – especially in healthcare or education provision – are
really vocations. Insofar as this means that such positions demand great skills and dedication on the part of those involved
it is clearly true, but this has nothing to do with the Christian
idea of vocation. With regard to one's job, and this is true of
all forms of employment, one earns a wage and has certain
rights and obligations. One has the right to a fair wage, to de-
cent working conditions, to holidays and free time and, if
these are denied, a right to strike. One's obligations are dictated
by contractual arrangements with employers. None of this is
true of a Christian vocation, since it is not a job but a way of
life. It is not based on contractual obligations but on personal
commitment. It does not lead to a fair wage for work done
but to the endless demand to give of oneself. It does not end
at 5 pm on a Friday evening but is ever present. And one does
not have the right to strike. A Christian vocation then is not a
job or a form of employment. It is the manner in which a particular individual is called within the Christian community to
live out his/her response to God's call.

When we speak of marriage as a vocation we do not mean
that an individual was predestined to marry his/her spouse
but that the relationship between God and the particular individual is inseparable from the reality of married life. The
relationship with God matures or declines in the context of

the particular commitment that the person has made to live in the married state. In other words, the most important realities in life through which we encounter the face of God – love and friendship, joy and heartbreak, maturing and ageing, sickness and death, sin and failure – are intimately intertwined with the experience of marriage. Similarly with those who are ordained or live under religious vows – they must work out their response to God's invitation in the particular context of their vocation.

Notice that these three vocations include the vast majority of adult members of the Catholic Church. But one notable group is missing – those who are single (unmarried) and are not ordained or members of religious orders. It is arguable that this is the most neglected group of people in the history of the church. They receive little of the ecclesial and other supports and recognition that are attached to being married, ordained or living in a religious community. The problem is, of course, that many single people will end up entering one of the three recognised vocations. And this has always been the problem – is a single life in itself truly a vocation? The answer is surely 'no'. Can it be a vocation? The answer is almost certainly 'yes'. For it to be so certain conditions, akin to those linked to the other vocations, would have to be met. It would need to be a long-term commitment entered into freely; the individual would have to be willing to put some of the energy and time that come from being single at the service of others, whilst the Christian community, for its part, would have to celebrate and support this form of vocation. In other words, for a single life to be a vocation it could not be just something that one slips into unplanned or unexpectedly; rather at a certain point in life one would have to make a definitive choice to live one's response to God in this way. Clearly, for this to happen the church will need to put in place some ritual which recognises and celebrates such a commitment. This may happen in the future. A beginning might be noted in the *Catechism of the Catholic Church* (paragraph 1658) which at least accepts the particular issues raised in the lives of single persons. Hopefully this might sow the seeds of further reflection on the nature of single life as a possible form of Christian vocation.

In the two chapters that constitute Part Three of this book, we devote our attention to marriage and holy orders. Single life is not treated of as the church has not recognised it formally as a vocation, nor do we deal with religious profession as, for varied historical reasons the analysis of which go beyond the bounds of this book, it is not a sacrament in the Catholic Church.

CHAPTER FIVE

Marriage

Is marriage a sacrament? The simple answer is 'yes'. But this deceptively simple answer raises a whole lot of other questions. Is marriage always a sacrament? The answer is 'no'; there are many examples – civil weddings, marriages between non-baptised spouses, marriages where one or both partners cannot celebrate the sacrament because of age or previous commitments or some other impediment. Was marriage always a sacrament? The answer is 'no'; it is only because of the life, death and resurrection of Christ that the natural union of man and woman has been transformed and raised to a higher plane. And the questions go on and on: what makes marriage a sacrament? Who can get married? Why are some marriages declared null? Even from this cursory analysis, one can begin to sense how complicated this whole issue can become. Indeed, it is so complex that some noted Christian thinkers have suggested that the church should withdraw from the area completely and leave it to the civil sphere of life. As attractive as this might sound, it is not a serious option. How could the church abandon what is the most important reality in the lives of the vast majority of its members? The task today is to restate the theology of marriage in a way that is true to Christian tradition and yet takes account of the 'signs of the times'. This chapter is an attempt to do just that.

Marriage in the scriptures
From the earliest texts of the Bible, marriage is endowed with

a special status. That God made them male and female means
that this distinction at the very heart of creation is divinely
willed. As man and woman joined together in wedlock, so too
Yahweh entered into a covenant with the people, but this was
a relationship characterised by the people's ingratitude and infidelity. And so the prophets, in speaking of Yahweh, use the
image of the lover who incessantly follows the unfaithful
beloved through wilderness and desert, mountain and plain,
enslavement and captivity, until the beloved would rediscover
her true identity.

The covenant was the relationship that bound God and
the people together. The early Christians began to speak of
the new covenant that emerged from the death and resurrection of Christ. Christ poured out his blood on the cross and
through this act of self-sacrifice he brought new life and hope
to the world. Because of their faith in the resurrection, the first
believers saw God as accepting Jesus' self-offering and they
looked forward to his return in glory. In the meantime they
had to face all sorts of interesting questions, not the least significant of which was: What does marriage mean in the light
of our faith in the death and resurrection of Christ? In order
to understand their perception of marriage, it is important to
bear a couple of things in mind. Marriage existed for centuries before Christianity so there was nothing new about it,
and the first believers thought that Christ's return was imminent. What really mattered was the latter, not the former. It
was important to ready oneself for the Lord's return and so
many believers abandoned all worldly concerns in the anticipation of an apocalyptic end to all material things. For some,
this included marriage. Thus in some of the writings of St
Paul marriage is looked upon as very definitely in second
place behind a life of personal commitment to the Lord.
Concerns about spouse and family do not compare with the
task of proclaiming the good news. Down through history

this line of thinking has dominated in the church's leadership which has generally perceived marriage as an inferior form of discipleship as compared to freely chosen virginity and celibacy. But early on, another strand of thought began to develop. As the first generation of believers themselves began to die, belief in the imminent return of the Lord declined. Christian communities were faced with how to cope with the world in the medium to longer term. It was during this period, towards the end of the first century and in the succeeding century, that the church put in place its structures of leadership and a new theology of marriage.

It is in a couple of short verses in the Letter to the Ephesians that we find an extraordinary claim about the meaning of marriage for Christians. Having quoted the famous verse from the book of Genesis – 'for this reason, a man must leave his father and mother and be joined to his wife, and the two will become one body' – the author goes on to say: 'this mystery has many implications; but I am saying that it applies to Christ and the church' (see Eph 5:31-32). The word 'mystery' is very significant in the Pauline corpus of writings. It refers to the whole mystery of what God reveals in Christ. In this passage marriage forms an integral part of that mystery. Far from being an insidious reality or a lesser form of discipleship, marriage is understood to be part of the relationship of Christ to his church. Christ's self-giving is prefigured and mirrored in the self-sacrifice that marriage entails. Notice too that the text refers to marriage going right back to the beginning. In other words, even before the coming of Christ marriage was already a symbol of the relationship of God to humanity. Given the times in which the text was written, this is indeed a notable claim. It is generally accepted that the Letter to the Ephesians was composed towards the end of the first century, quite some time after the death of Paul. At that time and throughout the next century, Christians were tempted to interpret their new faith through the lenses of various philosophies which were dominant in the world around them. The twin philosophies of manichaeism and dualism were hostile to anything material, including the human body and sexual intercourse. But the Pauline community from which this letter emerged rejected the idea that marriage and the human body were evil and that one would have to turn one's back on them in order to gain true spiritual enlightenment. Yet throughout the succeeding centuries, the debate over the Christian significance of marriage continued, since monasticism and celibacy dominated the popular mind as the only true path of discipleship.

Vatican II
In the *Constitution on the Church in the Modern World* (*Gaudium et Spes*, paragraphs 47-52) we find the most comprehensive statement that any church council ever made about marriage. Notably the idea of covenant is emphasised. Since medieval times, the dominant theology of marriage had centred on contract and on the obligations, particularly concerning child bearing, that this placed on the spouses. But Vatican II sounded a return to an older theology, that marriage was based more on relationship than contract. This brings one back inevitably to reflection upon the covenant and the theology of the Letter to the Ephesians. When one thinks of marriage as a covenant, one cannot but compare and contrast it with the relationship of God to the people. Only one word can describe the nature of the God of the old and new covenants – faithful, particularly in the midst of the faithlessness of the people. This is the God of love who, like a true lover, will ceaselessly seek out the beloved. Similarly, those who enter the covenant relationship of marriage will be asked to remain faithful even in the midst of great difficulties. Like the people of God of old, they have to go on a journey that will reveal all their weaknesses and failings and yet, even in the midst of these, they will be asked

to remain faithful, to trust in the God of the covenant when all else fails. This is the great story of human and divine love which ebbs and flows through human history. Undoubtedly Vatican II was right to contextualise marriage in this story, but the council also reaffirmed traditional teaching concerning commitment and indissolubility. It made clear that marriage between Christians is indeed a sacrament.

What makes marriage a sacrament?

Marriage is unique among the seven sacraments. In the other six, the ordinary minister is a bishop, priest or deacon (i.e. someone who is ordained), but in the case of marriage it is the man and woman who are getting married. The proof that we have failed to communicate this reality is obvious from the language that we use. We speak of the priest as having married a certain couple when this is not the case. The priest does not marry any couple; rather the man and woman marry each other. The task of the priest (or bishop or deacon) is to assist at the ceremony and bless the marriage. But with the complete domination of clergy in the church in recent centuries one could be forgiven for thinking that the key figure at many weddings is indeed the priest.

What do we mean by saying that the man and woman who are marrying each other are the ministers of the sacrament? It means that they confer the sacrament on each other through the mutual giving of consent. Without this consent there is no marriage. The role of the priest and the broader Christian community is secondary. What really matters is the consent of a man and woman to enter into a covenantal relationship with one another. To understand the significance of this, it is interesting to draw contrasts with other Christian churches. In the Eastern Orthodox Churches, the minister of marriage is the priest who, through crowning the man and woman, marries them. In most Protestant Churches there is a similar emphasis on the role of the cleric. But in the theology of the Catholic Church the consent of the couple constitutes the sacrament. That is why in the Catholic rite the man and woman are not declared to be husband and wife; nobody and no power can make a marriage except the consent of the couple. There are many implications that follow from this. One must remember, in reading these, that we are talking about marriages involving baptised Christians.

(a) Without true consent there is no marriage notwithstanding all appearances to the contrary. The two families can gather, the words can be spoken, the celebrations can be enjoyed but no marriage takes place unless consent is freely given.

(b) As ministers of the sacrament, the couple must intend to do that which the church does in the sacrament, i.e. they must intend to marry each other. Clearly on the day of the wedding nobody can appreciate the full personal, social and financial implications of marriage but the couple must intend to enter a lifelong relationship with one another.

(c) If one cannot give consent then one cannot be married in the Catholic Church. Quite a number of people cannot give the necessary consent. The obvious impediments to consent are age (one or other of the parties is too young), pressure to enter the marriage (which might be psychological, social or financial), or some medical conditions that mean a particular individual can never take on real responsibilities. There are other impediments defined in the church's law, the most controversial of which are an existing marriage bond, religious profession and ordination.

(d) Since it is the case that consent might not have been given (though the words were spoken), or that one of the parties was incapable of giving consent (though the words were spoken), then the church has to have a system in place whereby some marriages are declared invalid. This is usually called 'annulment'. The process through which a marriage is declared null will always be controversial as it almost inevitably involves judgments about the emotional maturity of those involved.

(e) Nobody can give another person permission to marry. The individual must decide. We used to speak a lot about 'letters of freedom' which priests were asked to give parishioners before marriage. Such letters did not bestow the freedom to get married; rather they were statements that, as far as the priest knew, this particular person was free to marry. The task of the priest is to establish, as best he can, that those who wish to get married are free to do so. If they are not, then he cannot give them such freedom.

(f) Because marriage is based on consent it is indissoluble. When two Christians freely promise to enter a relationship, their committed love is no longer just a private matter between them but it becomes part of the story of God's relationship with humanity. As the God of the covenants was faithful beyond what reason would demand, so too the marriage bond is raised to a new level. Authentic married love is caught up in divine love. This is what is meant by saying that marriage is a sacrament. The man and woman speak simple words, but the reality that they enter is far greater than themselves.

These implications raise as many questions as they answer. But maybe the most important one of all is this: Can consent be withdrawn? Clearly at a human level it often is. The bizarre level of marital breakdown and re-marriage in many Western countries demonstrates that large numbers of Christians believe that they can freely leave one marriage and enter another. And, of course, in civil law this is absolutely true. But this matter has little to do with civil law. It is a question of one's understanding of the relationship of God with humanity, of how one is going to live out one's discipleship of Christ as a vocation within the church. One can only understand the strict approach that the Catholic Church takes on the issue of dissolving marriages when one appreciates the theology of consent that we have been analysing here. Other churches take a more lenient view of things, but it is notable that their theology of marriage does not place the same emphasis on consent.

The necessity of faith

All sacraments demand and nourish faith. Without it they are meaningless. But, as ever, there is great difficulty in determining what faith is required and whether it exists or not. As a result, some pastors use a very strict criterion for admission to the sacraments, including marriage: one will only be admitted if one practises the faith frequently in the particular parish. With regard to the sacrament of marriage, a few simple points should be made. The faith required is essentially expressed through the giving of consent to one's partner rather than through weekly attendance at Sunday Mass. This amounts to a very significant act of faith in another person. If a baptised person is free to give such consent and desires to do so then, even if he/she does not practise the faith regularly, it is difficult to justify the refusal of some pastors to allow the ceremony to go ahead in their parish churches. It does, however, make a lot of sense to celebrate such a marriage outside of Mass. The normal context for a marriage between Catholics is the eucharist, but this need not be the case. When Catholics who have long since lapsed from attendance at Mass ask to get married in the church, then such marriages might not include a celebration of the eucharist. The reason for this is clear. The faith required for meaningful participation in the eucharist is of a different order from that necessitated by marriage. In the latter, one is asked to believe in the value of a human relationship based on trust and fidelity; in the former one is invited to believe that Christ is really present and to partake in the very life of God.

In order to nurture the faith of those preparing for marriage, parishes and dioceses should provide relevant preparation. This should emphasise the importance of consent. It should raise significant questions in the minds of those intending to get married. Am I too young to make such a commitment? Are my partner and I mature enough to set out on this path? Have I revealed my true self to the one I intend to wed? The participants might be encouraged to reflect upon the actual formula of consent. 'I take you as my husband/wife, for better or for worse, for richer or for poorer, in sickness and in health, all the days of my life.' Marriage is often for the better, for richer and experienced in good health. But at times it is for worse, it can lead to impoverishment and it will have to endure sickness. Those who intend to set out on this journey should have some sense that their commitment will be tested by life.

Most importantly of all, the actual ritual of marriage should be celebrated in such a way that its meaning and demands are clear, whilst giving true affirmation to the couple as they set out on the unknown journey.

The celebration of marriage

As marriage is the most important threshold that most believers will ever cross, it is surprising that the ritual is so simple. Leaving aside the celebration of the eucharist which accompanies many weddings, the actual rite of marriage is very short. Here it is in outline:

(i) Liturgy of the word
(ii) Liturgy of marriage
    address and examination
    consent of the couple
    blessing of rings, gold, silver etc.
    prayer of the newly married couple
    general intercessions
(iii) Nuptial blessing

This is the ritual celebration of marriage in the Catholic Church. Even within this simple ritual two things are much more important than the others – the address and examination and the giving of consent. The assistant (usually a priest or deacon or bishop, though it can be a delegated layperson) asks the man and woman if they have come freely and without pressure to get married. Then the couple gives consent. It is these two steps that constitute the sacrament of marriage. Everything else is secondary and should underpin the meaning of the giving of consent. Here are some pointers that might help:

(1) The rite allows for all sorts of regional variations in different parts of the world provided consent is asked for and given. Similarly it should be made clear to all those preparing for marriage that they do not have to accept various traditions which are not central to the rite, such as the giving away of the bride and particular forms of dress.

(2) Indigenous adaptations of the ritual could replace rings and money with more culturally nuanced symbols of wedlock.

(3) The couple should be involved in the preparation of all aspects of the ritual. This could include the composing of a prayer for the newly married.

(4) Because the words of consent are crucial they should be clearly heard. Couples should be encouraged to use the statement form of consent (where they say all of the words) rather than the interrogative form (where the priest says most of the words). After the words of consent have been spoken is a good time to play some reflective music so as to give all present a moment to savour the promises that have just been made.

(5) As at any sacramental gathering, the organisation of the available space is important. Given that the attendance at weddings will not normally fill the church building, steps should be taken to gather the congregation around the sanc-

tuary in a more intimate setting. Maximum audibility, visibility and participation are required. It can be beneficial to get the couple to face the congregation during the ritual of marriage. They will naturally feel shy in doing so but it clearly marks out the significance of the giving of consent. Furthermore, it will give the participants a real feeling of being pushed out to the threshold.

(6) Priests, or other assistants, should take care not to become the centre of attention. It is arguable that concelebration should be avoided at weddings as it only detracts from the centrality of the bride and groom. At any rate only the presiding priest/deacon should go forward for the examination and the giving of consent. The homily should take account of the fact that there are often many people present who do not regularly attend church. The care and solicitude of the Christian community for all people should be made clear.

Conclusion

The Christian understanding of marriage was fraught with difficulties from the beginning since the idea and reality of betrothal and wedlock long predated the emergence of the new faith. Right down to today, problems persist not just with marriage but with a whole range of associated issues like pre-marital sex, extra-marital affairs, divorce, gay/lesbian relationships amongst many others. Whilst these realities raise a whole range of moral questions and ethical challenges it is important to keep in mind that the basic theological principle concerning the nature of human relationships is premised upon consent and commitment. Where true consent and honest commitment are present, a relationship is surely Christian; where these are lacking, human dignity is undermined and people are abused. Fostering a sense of the value of consent and commitment is, then, an important pastoral goal in the life of the church. Nothing could be more important in this regard than supporting those who are preparing to get married. Those who freely embark on the journey of married life today are making an extraordinary act of faith in their partner and in God. It is now completely counter-cultural to enter into marriage with the intention of remaining faithful for life. All of the cultural undertones in Western countries suggest otherwise – sex is free, nobody could be expected to have only one partner in life, consent can be withdrawn whenever the individual gets tired or bored. In such a context it is probably true to say that those who freely enter the married state with open hearts and minds, and a desire to stand by their commitments through thick and thin, are among the most faithful of all God's people.

CHAPTER SIX

Holy Orders

One of the major debates of the reformation period centred on the nature of priesthood, whether indeed there should be priests at all. Today the idea of a church without priests, or at least without a set of people ordained and set apart for special ministry, seems almost absurd. Many Protestant Churches speak easily of ordination, priesthood, ministry and clergy; ordained ministers commonly dress in a manner that clearly distinguishes them from others who are baptised whilst much of the trenchant tone of the Reformation sounds like a distant echo. Does this mean that the Catholic Church's understanding of priesthood is now accepted by all? This is certainly not the case but it does mean that the need to justify the very existence of the priesthood is no longer a burning issue; the question today is not whether there should be a priesthood but rather what sort of priesthood we should have. One would imagine that a good place to start analysing this issue would be in contemporary theology. Unfortunately this is not the case. Our understanding of Christ, the church and the sacraments have undergone profound renewal due to modern theological research. But the same cannot be said of priestly life; we have oceans of canon law but still very little theology based on a renewed reading of the scriptures. Here we will highlight some themes that are pertinent in the development of a theology of the priesthood relevant to our times.

The three orders

There are three holy orders in the Catholic Church; that is why we speak of the sacrament of holy orders in the plural, since one can be ordained three times to the three orders of the diaconate (normally called deacons), the presbyterate (normally called priests) and the episcopate (normally called bishops). Bishops and presbyters both share in the priesthood whereas deacons do not. Both bishops and presbyters are ordained priests but according to Vatican II the fullness of the priesthood is found in the episcopate. This is an interesting statement for it means that the ministry of the priest/presbyter originates and culminates in the priestly ministry of the bishop. A clear change in emphasis from the Council of Trent was sounded here as the anti-Protestant polemics of the sixteenth century vested enormous power in the priest/presbyter, while a bishop was really understood as merely a more senior priest given special authority. That is why even today Catholics find it difficult to understand that a priest/presbyter is actually ordained as a bishop and so tend to use any verb except ordain, like consecrated, elevated and even coronated, for surely one can be ordained only once? The answer is definitely 'no'; in fact to become a bishop one must be ordained three times to each of the three orders. Becoming aware of the plurality of ministries already present in the three orders of the Catholic Church might sow the seeds of possible new horizons for ministries in the future.

Bishops

The Catholic Church is structured on the basis of dioceses overseen by bishops. The meaning of the word *episcopos* (bishop) is 'one who oversees'. From the first century onwards there were such overseers in the various churches, and in time their position became ever more important as the church began to see in them the guarantee of apostolic fidelity. The belief of the Catholic Church is that the first apostles chose successors to whom they handed on their teaching and power (especially the invocation of the Holy Spirit through the laying on of hands and the forgiveness of sin) and that these have been handed down faithfully from one generation to the next from the first apostles to our own time almost two thousand years later. Thus we speak of the apostolic link between us and the first apostles. In the Catholic Church this link is personified in the bishop whilst in most Protestant Churches the emphasis is placed on the scriptural word as the key to apostolic fidelity. In other words, most Protestants believe that the best way to follow the teaching of the apostles is to base one's life on the New Testament, whereas in the Catholic Church huge significance has always been attached to how that teaching has been handed down and interpreted by the successors of the apostles – the bishops.

The bishop is the key figure in the local church. In the Catholic Church these local or particular churches are called dioceses. It is a gross misunderstanding to perceive these dioceses or particular churches as branches or subsections of the universal church. Each diocese under a bishop is the one, holy, catholic and apostolic church in a particular place. It does not constitute only a bit of or a part of the church. It is the church in all of its reality in this place. Through its communion with other dioceses, it forms the Catholic Church. This idea of dioceses being truly the church is an important fact for the future as it bears within it the seeds of pastoral sensitivity to local issues and a proper balance in the relationship with Rome. Nobody is more important in these matters than the bishop. He is a member of the college of bishops, of that group who are responsible for sanctifying, teaching and ruling the church. Thus we speak of the collegiality of bishops, of their responsibility to maintain communion and fellowship between the various dioceses (particular churches) throughout the world. The head of that college is the Bishop of Rome, usually called the Pope. In the first few fractious centuries of Christian history, when there was painful division between the particular churches, the Bishop of Rome emerged as the focus of unity and communion in the universal church. Even today this remains the key element in the ministry of the Bishop of Rome – to foster communion and fellowship between the particular churches (dioceses) throughout the world. The Pope does not govern each diocese – that is the task of the local bishop. Rather the Pope personifies the universality of the church and he must ensure that the necessary bonds of faith, hope and charity are maintained and fostered among the particular churches. It is one of the great tragedies of Christian history that this very office has itself become the main focus of disputes and divisions. One of the most important tasks facing the Catholic Church today is to work out the proper relationship between Rome and the particular churches in dioceses throughout the world. This relationship has evolved historically and we can look forward to further evolution in the future. Such developments are important for the Catholic Church itself and are of crucial significance for its relationships with other Christian traditions.

A bishop must sanctify, teach and rule the particular church that he oversees. It is easy to understand then why bishops are generally conservative. They must conserve the teaching of the apostles which has been handed down from one generation to the next and they must maintain the bonds of communion with other dioceses both near and far. Such demanding tasks would make one naturally suspicious of changing fashions and mores that tend to be ephemeral and limited to specific geographical areas. But bishops must also lead their people to new horizons of faith and practice. They could learn much about this from the leaders of the church in the first century who adapted the church's life and language to varied religious, intellectual and political contexts. Today we speak of this as inculturation. The church will always have need of leaders who can speak the ancient message with new and creative voices.

Priests/Presbyters

The people we traditionally call priests should more exactly be called 'priests of the presbyteral order' since the category of priest also includes bishops. The Greek word *presbyteros* means 'elder'. To be a priest in the presbyteral order means that one is ordained to take a role of leadership in the community as a minister of word and sacrament. The reality of leader or elder is best expressed in the role of parish priest or pastor. The diocese of which the bishop is the 'overseer' is subdivided into parishes in which the parish priest has the responsibility to preach the word and celebrate the sacraments. Sometimes he might be supported in this by curates or assistant pastors.

Priests have a crucial role to play in the life of the church but, since the Second Vatican Council, important questions have been raised about the very nature of the priesthood. The focus of Vatican II on the centrality of episcopal ministry means that it can quite properly be spoken of as the 'council of bishops' since it renewed and amplified the life of bishops in the church. Similarly the role of the laity and those who live under religious vows was acknowledged and deepened. But the document on the life of priests/presbyters, *Presbyterorum Ordinis,* did not have the same cutting edge. As a result the new theological underpinning of bishops, laity and those living under religious vows was not replicated for the presbyterate. We have been living with the implications of this ever since as the new relationship between the priests/presbyters and the other groups are still being worked out. Priests entered Vatican II as the very heart beat of the church around

whom everything was organised and structured; they emerged
from the council into a different ecclesial setting where some
old certainties were beginning to wear very thin. Tension,
misunderstanding and downright hostility have characterised
many relationships as priests ceaselessly ask themselves: Who
are we? What is our role? Vatican II did not give theologically
significant answers to these questions but it opened up a whole
range of other issues which posed seemingly endless questions
for the presbyterate: What is the new relationship with the
laity? What are the priorities in ministry? What exactly should
one do from day to day? The renewal initiated at the council
found its focus for those living under religious vows in a redis-
covery of the charisms of their founders; for the baptised
there were newly emerging theologies giving people a real
sense of the meaning of their baptism; for bishops there was
an edifying vision of their apostolic calling; but for priests
there was little but the chilly words of the code of canon law.
No matter how much significance one attaches to law, it is
not the most potent motive force for creating the future;
theologies which both challenge and affirm the presbyterate
are required to enable priests of the future rediscover who
they are in the life of the baptismal community.

Christian priesthood means nothing apart from Jesus who
is called the Christ. Two thousand years ago he preached the
dawning reign of God. He wasn't a member of the priestly
caste of his time but that didn't stop him from preaching the
good news, healing the sick, bringing liberty to captives, comforting the broken-hearted and bringing new sight to the
blind. Jesus' identity did not come from being born into a
priestly caste but it was forged in his interaction with the one
he called 'Abba' and in his encounter with friends and foes on
the highways and byways of Galilee. Through prayer, reflection and human encounter Jesus discovered the divine depths
of life. All Christians are asked to follow him on this path but

priests have a particularly significant role to play. They are asked to preside at the liturgical gatherings of the community, to preach the gospel and to lead people through prayer and sacrament to an ever deeper encounter with the divine depths of our lives. These are demanding tasks. Nobody could even begin to fulfill them in a meaningful way without serious dedication to prayer, reading and self-reflection. Without these a priest's ministry is likely to spiral into a decline of empty repetitions, hollow encounters and pious rhetoric.

One shouldn't conclude, however, that there is only one way of being a priest in the tradition of Jesus of Nazareth. There are as many ways of living priestly life as there are priests in the world. Every priest has the right to forge his identity in the context in which he finds himself. Some will want to live in a counter-cultural manner through wearing distinctive dress, living frugally and standing apart from many social activities. Others prefer to be more like a leaven in the world – alive and active but not readily distinguishable from everybody else. One way or the other, the task is always to proclaim the dawning reign of God as Jesus did.

That which distinguishes Christian faith from other religions is belief in the Trinity and the incarnation. Think about these wonderful doctrines for a moment. In God's own life there is relationship; God is one but not solitary. In the incarnation God embraced humanity in all its beauty and wickedness and began to transform it from within. These doctrines, the very heartbeat of Christianity, should tell us much about priesthood. The priest's life should, like that of the Triune God, be characterised by life-giving and sustaining relationships and, like Christ, the priest should be immersed in the tangled human world of good and evil, hope and despair, life and death. Priests must try to wander around the sacred spaces in the world and in the soul; they should visit the corners of brokenness and emptiness and yet hear the call to transcendence; they should hope against hope and, in a very traditional language, they should know the depth of their own sinfulness and the breadth of divine love. And then, in the tradition of Christ himself, their words might indeed be redemptive and salvific.

Sacrifice is one of the defining aspects of all religions. Priesthood and sacrifice are inseparable. The priest is the one who offers the sacrifice, the altar is the place where the offering is made and the victim is that which is offered. In ancient pagan religions the first-born was sacrificed to the gods – originally this was a human, later an animal or the first fruits of the harvest. In the Jewish tradition the priests oversaw the temple sacrifices. But it is noteworthy that the early Christians did not adopt the language and symbols of the Jewish priesthood. The first believers attached numerous titles to Jesus but they were very slow to speak of him as the new high priest. This language was developed in the Letter to the Hebrews. The letter was written after the destruction of the temple in 70AD and it addressed a real issue for the Jewish Christians who had remained faithful to the temple sacrifices – what is the meaning of priesthood once the temple had disappeared? Clearly there was a problem, since Jesus was no priest in the ordinary Jewish sense. He hadn't been born of the right stock and not alone had he not been a priest in the Jerusalem temple but he had attacked it with some fury. As a result the Letter to the Hebrews re-interpreted the meaning of the priesthood. Christ is spoken of as the priest and the victim since he sacrificed his own life on a new altar – the cross. Therefore Christians came to understand Christ as the new high priest, the one who offers the sacrifice, and as the victim, for he was the one who was offered. Thus the ancient tradition of sacrifice is given a new interpretation – the demand for self-sacrifice.

A key element in the renewal of priestly life will be self-sac-

rifice. The great temptation is towards comfortable bachelor-
hood. Such a lifestyle has little to say to anyone. It needs to be
thrown into serious question before it quenches the spirit of
the gospel. One way of re-kindling this spirit is to withdraw
to the edge, the threshold, the desert. The encounter with life
on the edge, the periphery, the margins, remains the key to
unleashing the powers of renewal in the lives of individuals
and in the lives of great institutions like the churches.
Creativity emerges from the margins. Artists, writers, philoso-
phers, mystics, go to the edge, the margins of their experience,
and from there they interrogate the presumptions upon
which our world is built. Priests need to withdraw to the edge
too in order to revisit the wellsprings that nourish Christian
faith. They can do so by participating in a serious retreat,
going on sabbatical, volunteering for work in impoverished
communities at home or abroad. Such experiences, often demanding great self-sacrifice, are the food of the soul.

This theology of sacrifice found its most powerful expression in the rule concerning priestly celibacy. The tradition of
celibate priests has a long and rich history in the Catholic
Church. Only those with a very biased view of things would
question the contribution that a celibate priesthood has made
to prayer and pastoral care, to missionary outreach and
Christian living. But the rise of modern psychology and the
emergence of the sexual revolution, which have engrossed
Western civilisation since the 1960s, naturally throw such a
tradition into question. We now know far more than previous
generations did about friendship and emotional maturity,
sexuality and personal identity, childhood experiences and
problems in later life, homosexuality and homophobia, child
sexual abuse and manipulative relationships. The world of
sexual innocence has been shattered. Things will never be the
same again. It is as if a still pond of water has been upset and
all the material that rested at the bottom has begun to rise to

the surface. The reality of child sexual abuse perpetrated by some clergy and religious has changed people's perception of celibacy. It probably was the case that most people could never understand celibacy as an option for life and so they elevated those who chose such a path onto a pedestal of purity and innocence that they didn't share. Now they know that those who try to live celibate lives are as sexually and emotionally complicated as everybody else.

The celibate priesthood has a future since its ranks include people of extraordinary emotional maturity, generosity and other-centredness. But there is no reversing the insights of psychology or the power of the sexual revolution. We know that life cannot be lived in a humane way without intimacy and friendship, that celibacy can be an escape mechanism from these realities, but that it can also be lived in a way which overcomes isolation and fear. As ever, it is probably a good idea to look back to the scriptures. The life of Jesus makes no sense apart from very particular people: Mary, Martha and Lazarus who lived in the poor village of Bethany, John the beloved disciple and the other women and men whom he encountered on the way. Wherever the church learned in later times to mistrust the value of friendship and intimacy, it certainly wasn't from deep reflection on the life of Jesus of Nazareth.

Deacons

The third order of the three holy orders is the diaconate. It has had a troubled history. For a thousand years prior to Vatican II there were no permanent deacons in the Catholic Church. Throughout the first millennium of the Christian era, the priesthood grew in stature and power to such an extent that the diaconate became all but obsolete. In the second millennium the diaconate became nothing more than a stepping stone to the priesthood. Before one could be ordained a priest in the presbyteral order one had first to be ordained a deacon. This remains the case today. But Vatican II introduced an important reform when it set in motion the process by which the permanent diaconate was restored in the life of the church. Thus today we speak of the transitional diaconate (those who will shortly be ordained as priests) and the permanent diaconate (those who will remain as deacons for the rest of their lives).

The Greek word *diakonia* means 'service'. Thus deacons are called to serve the Christian community. They do this through preaching the word of God, baptising new members of the church, assisting at marriages, presiding at funerals and reaching out to those in need. The re-establishment of the permanent diaconate in the Catholic Church has given new life to this ancient ministry. The fact that married men can be ordained to this ministry means that it opens the door to ordination for many who were previously excluded.

Ordination ceremonies

The various rites of ordination are amongst the most potent rituals of the Catholic Church. The rites were revised in the light of the Second Vatican Council. Through the prayer of consecration and the laying on of hands by the bishop, the individual member of the Christian community is ordained to one of the three orders. The three ceremonies have much in common. Candidates for the diaconate and presbyterate are presented to the bishop and the assembly by a relevant person (maybe the parish priest or a representative from the seminary where the candidate trained). The bishop asks if they have been found worthy and the assembly expresses its consent. This latter aspect is interesting, for the reality is that the community is not involved in making any judgment on the suitability of the candidate. But the survival of this ancient tradition in the rite is welcome since the possibility remains that at some time in

the future the community might again have a more significant role in choosing its own leaders. At any rate this is a good
time in the rite for someone who knows the candidate to
speak of his Christian maturity and suitability for the ministry
upon which he is about to embark; this obviously implies that
if the candidate is immature or unsuitable then he should not
be presented for ordination. In the case of the episcopate, the
one to be ordained is presented to the assembled bishops and
the community and the apostolic mandate (a letter from the
Pope approving the individual for ordination as bishop of the
particular diocese) is read. In all three rites, the candidate is
then examined in public before the gathered community.
Then he lies prostrate while the community intercedes for the
gift of the Holy Spirit. This is followed by the key moment in
the rite with the laying on of hands and the prayer of consecration. Since bishops and presbyters are given a share in the
priesthood of Christ, they are anointed with chrism (deacons
are not so anointed because they are not ordained to the
priesthood). Finally, the newly ordained are presented with
symbols and insignia proper to their office – a bishop receives
the gospels, a ring, a mitre and a staff; a presbyter is clothed in
a chasuble and stole and presented with bread and wine; a
deacon is vested with a dalmatic and stole and is given the
gospels. The rite closes with the kiss of peace.

These sacramental rituals clearly constitute rites of passage
through which an individual is bestowed with a new office in
the Christian community. Given the importance of these
ministers in the life of the community, it is surely welcome
that most ordinations now take place in an active parish church
and, in the case of the episcopal rite, in the local cathedral.

A priestly community

One cannot understand the episcopate, presbyterate and diaconate without the community of believers. However small

or disorganised, however persecuted or comfortable, however strong or weak, however traditional or prophetic, however active or dormant, the community of believers is the primordial reality in Christianity. All else only makes sense as emerging from and existing for the community. The single greatest threat to Christian faith in the Western world is the growing privatisation of life. Homes are becoming zones of seclusion; worse, the inhabitants want it that way. The withdrawal into our living rooms, where the television can become the key access to the world, inevitably fragments the communal world that we once inhabited. The onslaught of the internet and cyberspace will offer opportunities for new types of cyber communities where one's neighbour will not be defined geographically in terms of traditional space and time but through cyber space and time. In this world of technological revolution, sacramental space is squeezed and the interaction of community, religious belief and ritual is thrown into serious question. Whatever the merits of privatisation in business and commerce, it is a fatal flaw in religious sensibility. It is difficult to speak in such a world of the true meaning of Christianity; people are probably happy enough to receive the body of Christ but they have little taste for that same body as encountered in the community of believers.

The church is properly understood to be the people of God, the body of Christ and the temple of the Holy Spirit. Such an understanding should awaken in each member of the church a sense of his/her baptismal dignity. But sadly this has seldom been the case. The ministries of bishops, priests and deacons evolved over the first few centuries of Christian history. In time the priesthood became the most important office in the Catholic Church. As ever, the great temptation was to abuse power, to become one who dominated and around whom everything else revolved. Down through history, the dominance of the priest continued to grow to such an extent that one could be forgiven for thinking that in the post-Tridentine church the community existed for the priest. The laity became little more than passive observers and listeners in a clerical structure. But the Second Vatican Council gave fresh impetus to an old doctrine – that all the baptised share in the priesthood of Christ. Thus part of the task of the future is to awaken Christian communities to their priestly character through fostering charisms and new ministries to give expression to this priestly dimension.

It is easy to be clear about what this does not mean. It does not mean that everyone who is baptised is also ordained as a priest. The ministerial priesthood of word and sacrament remains clearly distinct. But it does mean that all baptised Christians are called to share in the priesthood of Christ. They can do so in different ways but the ultimate goal is that the charisms freely bestowed by the Spirit of God should be placed at the service of all. From a Christian perspective, charisms or gifts are not just personal talents, they are intended for the up-building of the community. They vary enormously and are literally innumerable, but to give a flavour of how gifted the Christian community is, here are just a few: consoling the bereaved, healing the sick, comforting the lonely, encouraging the downcast, embracing poverty, reaching out to the addicted, being celibate, counselling, praying, leading, forgiving, teaching, believing, hoping, loving. These charisms are present in abundance; it is the task of a priestly community to affirm them, harness them and challenge those who have been so blessed to put their gifts at the service of the Christian community. This has been one of our great failures to date. With the clericalisation of ministry, the baptised have lost all sense of their priestly character.

The Christian priestly communities which emerge in the cities of the future will be counter-cultural, creating sacred sacramental spaces in the midst of urban anonymity, sowing the seeds of the kingdom of God in soil that appears hostile, disturbing the cosy conscience of the consumer. There are a few certainties about such communities: they will not be a 'one man show' where all power is vested in the parish priest. The great temptation for the priest is to think that he is on his own and then to lapse into either frustration (where nothing gets done) or dictatorship (where virtually everyone gets alienated). Instead he must cultivate a sense of shared responsibility. In the future there will be a plurality of ministries and it is probably the case that we will have to imagine new structures apart from the parish to incarnate the church in the city. The best priests have always devoted their energies, wherever they found themselves, to building community; that task has not changed but it cannot be undertaken alone. The days of the priestly 'lone ranger' are numbered.

The key question which faces the church in the Western world today is not 'who should be ordained?' but 'what does it mean to be baptised?' Since Vatican II we have made a lot of mistakes in attempting to answer that question. We fell into the trap of equating lay participation/ministry with sanctuary ministry. Lectors (readers at Mass) and extraordinary ministers of the eucharist became the be all and end all of lay participation. To reduce lay participation in the church to these very limited roles is essentially to empty it of all significance. It must be expanded to include parish catechists, family and bereavement counsellors, chaplains (though maybe we need a different title) for schools and hospitals and prisons. When one adds to this all the tasks currently performed by priests but which have nothing directly to do with priestly ministry – from representation on school boards to organising parish finances and, on a different level, from representing the church at international gatherings to staffing the Vatican's diplomatic corps – one can see that there is a lot to be done that need not be done by priests.

Is it true, as some commentators suggest, that there is a real hostility to change amongst the clergy? More importantly, is it true that younger clergy are even less interested in a new future than their older confrères? Priests need to realise that the days of lording it over the people are gone. What the church needs most of all today are people who can articulate the significance of Christian faith, who can speak a word of healing and hope, in a secular but broken world. It has little need of those who can only parrot doctrine and moral absolutes. The most important development in twentieth-century thought was the quantum leap whereby physicists moved from the world of Newtonian certainty to the unpredictable universe of subatomic physics. The Catholic Church needs a quantum leap of faith to bring it to new horizons. While cherishing many of the things it holds dear, it needs to abandon some old attachments in the embrace of an unpredictable future. If its clergy are not up to this task then they risk being left behind in a lonely ghetto.

Conclusion

The priest has a crucial role to play in the life of every Christian community. As a minister of word and sacrament, he leads the assemblies of believers when they gather for their sacramental rituals. The great occupational hazard of such ministry is that repetition can sap the energy and insight which are so necessary in the leader of the assembly. A priest encounters people at critical threshold moments in their lives – birth, death, serious illness, marriage and at times of reconciliation. He needs to develop a sensitivity for symbol and ritual so that his words and actions bring healing and hope into people's lives.

In chapter one we outlined the various ways in which a community could awaken a sense of the edge/threshold in sacramental celebrations, yet without doubt the priest is central to this process. He must act as a leader in this area because lay people will not feel that they can take the initiative in sacramental renewal. A significant number in any parish may have worthwhile ideas about how to celebrate the sacraments more fruitfully as thresholds, yet their efforts are destined to flounder without the good will and support of the priest.

A sacramental people needs to encounter, through word and symbol, those Christian realities which can give meaning and perspective to our lives. Simply, we need to experience our sacraments as thresholds. Our primitive forebears celebrated the transformations of the seasons and the cosmos and the passages of life and death. Woven into this rich tapestry of ritual and symbol is a narrative which demands that we embrace the thresholds that we constantly encounter in life. Remember the threshold is the place of perspective and change, renewal and critique. Our sacraments will speak to the lives of those in our communities when they too become thresholds, truly doors which open onto the very life of God.

Contemporary life is weighed down by the demands of materialism and the fruits of a consumerism which has only bequeathed isolation and anxiety. We have never been in such need of the renewing qualities of ritual and a definitive responsibility lies with priests to awaken a sense of the edge/threshold. The contemporary role of the church may well be to serve the needs of a society that is illiterate in the grammar of ritual and symbol. Of all the social institutions, it is the Catholic Church which is competent in ritual and of all times, it is our era which begs such a proficiency.

Part Four

Being a Sacramental People

In this chapter we describe many different rituals. Some of the reflective texts used in these rituals can be found in the Appendix. Our intention is that parishes, schools, retreat teams or other communities might adapt these texts and rituals to their own needs. We give a few suggestions as to their likely use but these are only broad guidelines. It is more important to use your imagination in adapting these ideas to your own context. Remember the basic premise of this book is that the key symbols of the sacraments are more powerful than we ordinarily believe and that if we allow them to speak they could become a focus for renewal in the church. Interacting with symbols breathes new life into our faith as without them it is little more than an intellectual claim, but through them it becomes incarnate and communal. The only way to see if this works is actually to try it. You might be surprised by what you discover. Remember to keep in mind the issues concerning rituals that were discussed in Chapter One.

1. Landscapes and Seascapes

In this ritual we visit significant geographical sites which help to awaken a sense of life on the threshold. In the text that follows we mention hills, monasteries, wells, seashore and tombs. The ritual is easily adapted for use in one or more of these locations. Ideally a group of participants should spend a day walking from one site to the other.

On the Mountaintop
The participants gather in a circle facing inwards.

Leader: Why have people always come to the mountaintop?
    Down below on the plains and in the valleys life is familiar, routine and often banal. In the city the streets are thronged and things move quickly. In our homes the television is ever present. In the car our space is cramped. In the workplace there is little time to do what we want.

    But here on the mountaintop life is unfamiliar, different and refreshing. The ascent can be slow and difficult yet we always struggle to the top to touch again the vast emptiness, to see again the distant horizons, to taste again the unfettered wind, to smell again the fragrant air, to hear again the sounds of silence.

    Look around you. Touch the emptiness. Look at the horizons. Taste the wind. Smell the air. Listen to the silence.

Depending on the place and the amount of time available the participants should now be given some time to wander freely. When the people re-gather they should form a circle again but this time facing outwards. Then the following pieces of scripture are read.

Reader 1: I lift up my eyes to the mountains:
From where shall come my help?
My help shall come from the Lord
Who made heaven and earth.
(Psalm 121)

Reader 2: Go up on the high mountain,
joyful messenger to Sion.
Shout with a loud voice
joyful messenger to Jerusalem.
Shout without fear
say to the towns of Judah
'Here is your God'.
(Isaiah 40:9)

Leader: The mountain is holy ground; it is sacred space. Moses encountered the Lord Yahweh on the mountaintop. Down below the people strayed, seduced by the lure of false gods. They forgot who they truly were and became immersed in the world and its attractions. They would have to learn over and over again to climb the mountain of the Lord and to seek God's ways. We too must visit these holy places to rediscover the truth of who we are as God's own people, a holy nation, a royal priesthood, a people set apart to sing the praises of God. Before we return to the valleys and plains, to the cities and the suburbs, to our cars and homes, we anoint one another with oil of gladness to strengthen us on life's journey.

Each participant is anointed with oil.

Leader: Remember that this is a holy place, remember who you are.

Participant: On the mountain Yahweh provides. (Genesis 22:14)

The participants descend the hill or mountain. At a suitable location at the bottom they gather again in a circle.

Leader: Look again to the mountaintop. Remember this is a sacred place.

All recite or sing together:

The Lord is my shepherd,
There is nothing I shall want.
Fresh and green are the pastures where he gives me repose;
Nears restful waters he leads me to revive my drooping spirit.

He guides me along the right path,
He is true to his name.
If I should walk in the valley of darknesss no evil would I fear.
You are there with your crook and your staff,
With these you give me comfort.

You prepare a banquet for me in the sight of my foes,
My head you have anointed with oil,
My cup is overflowing.
Surely goodness and kindness shall follow me all the days of my life.
In the Lord's own house shall I dwell forever and ever.

At the Monastery

The people might gather in the vicinity of a living monastery or in the ruins of a long since extinct one.

Leader: When Samuel was a boy it was rare for Yahweh to speak in those days. Yet Yahweh called out to Samuel but the boy did not understand that Yahweh calls. When he heard his name being called he ran to Eli and said, 'Here I am' because he did not understand. Then Eli told him the truth and when Yahweh called the third time Samuel replied, 'Speak, Yahweh, your servant is listening.' Then

Yahweh spoke to Samuel and his life was never the same afterward.

Reader 1: When we are old enough we understand that sometimes we must let go of our plans and let God be the God of our future:
'I tell you most solemnly
when you were young
you put on your own belt
and walked where you liked;
but when you grow old
you will stretch out your hands,
and somebody else will put a belt round you
and take you where you would rather not go.' (Jn 21:18)

Leader: Look around you at these hallowed walls. This sacred place is replete with the memories of those who have left the world to journey into the mystery of the inner self, supported by a community of faith. Like Samuel these servants learned to listen to the voice of the spirit of God and relinquish the call of the spirit of the world.

Read: The spirit of God and the spirit of the world.
Two readers are needed, one reads the spirit of the world and the other the spirit of God. In each case the spirit of the world comes first followed within a couple of seconds by the spirit of God; there is then a substantial pause (10-15 seconds) before moving on. Ideally the two readers should stand at opposite ends of the relevant space.

(1) The spirit of the world says that externals are all important – looks, property, possessions. You are what you have.

(2) The spirit of God says that your looks and appearance can be very deceptive. You must look into the heart, into the depth of life to see who we really are.

(1) The spirit of the world says that life is a test and success is everything. It abhors failure and disappointment.

(2) The spirit of God says that failure can be more important than success. We can learn much even from the sad and more difficult times.

(1) The spirit of the world says that the great problems – unemployment, ecology, violence – have nothing to do with me. I've just got to mind my own patch.

(2) The spirit of God says that I am responsible for everyone, everywhere, at all times. There are no strangers in God's eyes.

(1) The spirit of the world says that love is about things going well, in accord with my plans.

(2) The spirit of God says that love is about giving of myself, even when I feel that I cannot.

(1) The spirit of the world says that there is no such thing as forgiveness because there is no such thing as sin.

(2) The spirit of God says that forgiveness is the greatest reality that we know. We sin, we fail, yet we can be freed to go on.

(1) The spirit of the world says that honesty and commitment are impossible and don't really exist.

(2) The spirit of God says that honesty and commitment are the only things that really matter in the end.

(1) The spirit of the world says that the sick and the disabled are not really alive. Sickness and disability are disastrous.

(2) The spirit of God says that the sick and the disabled are often those who are most alive for they know their dependence; they know that life is not in their control.

(1) The spirit of the world says that death is the end of life and proves that life is futile.

(2) The spirit of God says that death is not the end of life as the great spirit present in us is not extinguished but transformed.

Leader: We have all made choices and each in his or her way has listened to the call of God. We have been called as men or women and given the gifts and talents to answer the call of our baptism to become truly Christian.

Rituals should regenerate and give people new energy. There might be an opportunity now to use the rites of affirmation on pp. 147-150. These rites are intended to highlight the gifts of various adults within the community: women, men, priests. Each group (women, men, priests) is called forward separately. They go to the front of the group where they stand facing the leader/elders whilst the others remain seated. Then the texts are read aloud by the leader/elders. Immediately afterwards they place an open Bible over the head of each individual and say: 'God's word has been sown in your heart. You are God's word.'

Around the Well

Leader: Water is the source of all life and it was through water that we entered a life of faith in Christ. When we revisit water we revisit the sacrament of our baptism, a sacrament that we may have long forgotten.

Read the following text. Two readers are required.

1. At the very dawn of creation God's Spirit breathed on the waters.

2. In the beginning God created the heavens and the earth. Now the earth was a formless void, there was darkness over the deep, and God's Spirit hovered over the water.

1. The waters of the great flood brought an end to sin and a new beginning of goodness.

2. I establish my covenant with you: no thing of flesh shall be swept away again by the waters of the flood. There shall be no flood to destroy the earth again.

1. Through the waters of the Red Sea God led Israel out of slavery.

2. Yahweh drove back the sea with a strong easterly wind all night, and he made dry land of the sea. The waters parted and the children of Israel went on dry ground right into the sea, walls of water to right and left of them.

1. In the waters of the Jordan Jesus was baptised by John and anointed with the Spirit.

2. Immediately afterwards the Spirit drove him out into the wilderness and he remained there for forty days, and was tempted by Satan. He was with the wild beasts, and the angels looked after him.

1. When Jesus hung on the cross blood and water flowed from his side.

2. When they came to Jesus, they found he was already dead, and so instead of breaking his legs one of the soldiers pierced his side with a lance and immediately there came out blood and water.

1. In baptism we were baptised with water in the name of the Father and of the Son and of the Holy Spirit.

2. When we were baptised in Christ Jesus we were baptised in his death; in other words, when we were baptised we went into the tomb with him and joined him in death, so that as Christ was raised from the dead by the Father's glory, we too might live a new life.

The leader sprinkles everyone with water saying:
    You were baptised in the name of the Father and of the Son and of the Holy Spirit.
Alternatively people come forward and bless themselves with the water saying:
    I believe in God the Father and the Son and the Holy Spirit.

As people are being sprinkled with water there is music or song.
The last aspect of the ritual is the renewal of baptismal promises:

Leader: Do you believe in God the creator of light and darkness, land and sea, heaven and earth, woman and man?
All: We do.

Leader: Do you cherish and protect the earth as God's creation?
All: We do.

Leader: Do you appreciate the gift of water which endlessly
renews and sustains life?
All: We do.

Leader: Do you give thanks for the spring and the summer,
the sowing and the harvest, the sun and the moon, the
wind and the rain, the mountain top and the sea shore?
All: We do.

Leader: Do you believe that in the midst of a beautiful world
we, like Adam and Eve, live in the shadow of temptation
and evil?
All: We do.

Leader: Do you reject all that is evil?
All: We do.

Leader: Do you reject injustice, hatred, despair and bigotry?
All: We do.

Leader: Do you reject all that undermines and destroys the
gift of life?
All: We do.

Leader: Do you believe that Jesus Christ is the saviour of the
world?
All: We do.

Leader: Do you believe that Jesus died for us on Calvary and was raised from the dead?
All: We do.

Leader: Do you believe that in baptism you became followers of Jesus?
All: We do.

Leader: Do you believe that when you were anointed with oil in baptism you received the gift of God's Spirit?
All: We do.

Leader: Do you believe that God's Spirit is present in humanity and that our destiny is to share fully in God's own life?
All: We do.

Leader: Do you accept the Christian identity that was given to you in your name at baptism?
All: We do.

Leader: Do you accept that your faith can only be lived with others in a Christian community?
All: We do.

Leader: Do you believe that the church, a community of saints and sinners, is the temple of God's presence in the world?
All: We do.

Leader: Do you take responsibility for the future well-being of the church?
All: We do.

Leader: Do you believe in the final triumph of Christ over sin, light over darkness, truth over lies, hope over despair, good over evil and life over death?
All: We do.

Leader: Do you today, in the presence of fellow believers, confirm the meaning and implications of your baptism?

All: We do.

Leader: Do you now promise to live your life in accordance with the Christian faith which we have professed together?

All: We do.

Leader: Then may God bless you and strengthen you as you bear witness to your faith.

By the Shore

Leader: Many years ago our forebears cried out to God to save them from slavery. Moses led them out of Egypt to the shore of the Red Sea. Pursued by the Egyptian army the people feared death and cried out in their anguish 'Better to work for the Egyptians than die in the wilderness'. In the midst of unbelief God stretched back the waters and the people walked from the shore, from slavery, full of joy and faith in God.

There are dark places in life when we lose faith and in hopelessness would prefer to die in the wilderness of our own despair.

All present should be asked to take off their shoes and enter the water.

Leader: By the shores of the Sea of Galilee Jesus called his first disciples. Later they left the same shore and the wind rose and the storm lashed their modest fishing boat. Like their forebears at the shore of the Red Sea they despaired until Jesus calmed the waters and asked them 'Where is your faith?'

In the midst of the crises, temptations, turmoils and sufferings of modern life, we may ask: 'Where is our God?' Our God says: 'Where is your faith?'

Once after his death, Christ beckoned his disciples in from the Sea of Galilee. There they were filled with faith in the risen Christ. Look now at the sea and remember your faith in the Christ who saves and in the God who first spoke to Moses saying: 'I have observed the misery of my people who are in Egypt ... I know their sufferings and I have come down to deliver them'.

Through the waters of the Red Sea and the waters of our baptism and from the shores of the Sea of Galilee, we are called to a discipleship of faith. Just as Christ demanded of his disciples by the shore so it is demanded of you today:

As the following text is read to each person they are invited to walk in from the sea:

(Name) when you were young
you walked where you liked
but when you are old
you will be taken where you would rather not go.

Visiting a Tomb or Graveyard

Leader: It is part of the rhythm of human life that something must die before new life can begin. Here in this place of dying and death we are reminded of the need to let go of those memories which prevent us from experiencing new life in Christ. Life can bring us to places of great hurt and tragedy and these experiences can hold us bound in anger and resentment. Human life is wounded, broken and at times torn apart, but just as we were baptised into Christ's death so too we were baptised into new life with him. Easter tells us that we are called to live a life of sacrifice and so we must learn to let go of that which prevents us from experiencing the fullness of Christian life.

The following text, or something similar might be used:

Lord God help me to let go.
Life is an endless process of letting go;

In our birth we had to let go of the security of our mother's womb and emerge into a strange world;

In adolescence we let go of the innocence of childhood;

All of us have to let go of home, parents must let go of their children and children must let go of their parents;

Throughout life as we grow and mature we must continually let go of opinions, jobs, good health and ultimately of the idea that we are in control.

And, of course, in death we must let go of those we love.

Between womb and tomb life is an endless process of letting go.

Come, Holy Spirit, help me to let go so that even when the letting go is tearful and sad it will awaken me to the mystery and wonder of life.

Life is the greatest gift we have received and we must in the end let go of this gift.

We must let go of the past to let God be the God of the future.

A scriptural text for this rite can be taken from any of the passion narratives and it is important that these texts play a central role to stress the paschal nature of this dying in Christ. The shadow of the words of St Paul should envelop this place; 'when we were baptised in Christ Jesus we were baptised in his death..' (Rom 6:3). One possibility then is to read the text of Ecclesiastes 3:1-8:

For everything there is a season, and a time for every matter under heaven:

a time to be born, and a time to die;

a time to plant, and a time to pluck up what is planted;

a time to kill, and a time to heal;

a time to break down, and a time to build up;

a time to weep, and a time to laugh;

a time to mourn, and a time to dance;

a time to throw away stones, and a time to gather stones
together;
a time to embrace, and a time to refrain from embracing;
a time to seek, and a time to lose;
a time to keep, and a time to throw away;
a time to tear, and a time to sew;
a time to keep silence, and a time to speak;
a time to love, and a time to hate;
a time for war, and a time for peace.

*If the group are visiting a particular grave they might gather
around it and recite the following text:*

We are not afraid of dying to the old,
We are not afraid of giving birth to what is new,
We are not afraid of planting,
We are not afraid of uprooting what has been planted,
We are not afraid of searching,
We are not afraid of keeping or throwing away,
We are not afraid of tears or mourning,
We are not afraid of laughter.

*Finally it should be noted that some soft singing or humming in
the background can be very evocative.*

2. Reconciliation service

Aspects of the following texts could be used in the celebration of rite two of the sacrament of reconciliation. Ideally those who attend this service should sit in a circle. There should be two lecterns within the circle facing one another. Suitable music or songs can easily be woven into this service.

Leader: To be Christian is to be a member of a community of saints and sinners. In this community we often fail to live up to the meaning of our baptism and to live out what the eucharist demands of us. Let us listen to God's word as it speaks to us today.

A couple of suitable scripture texts should now be read or the following texts from St Paul might be used. There should be two readers reciting the texts alternatively with a short pause between each one. The two readers should stand at the two lecterns.

(1) The word of God cuts more finely than a double edged sword. It cuts between the marrow and the bone so that the truth can emerge.

(2) What we preach is Christ crucified; a scandal for Jews and folly for Greeks, but for us who believe, the wisdom and glory of God. For God's foolishness is wiser than human wisdom, and God's weakness is stronger than human strength.

(1) It is when I am weak that I am strong, for I feel the power of Christ shining through my human weakness.

(2) I, Paul, appointed by God to be an apostle, send greetings to the church of God in Corinth, to the holy people of Jesus Christ who are called to take their place among all the saints everywhere. May God our Father and the Lord Jesus Christ send you grace and peace.

(1) Nothing can ever come between us and the love of God made visible in Christ Jesus our Lord. No angel, no power, no division, no fear can ever separate us from the love of God.

(2) The blessing cup that we bless is a communion with the blood of Christ and the bread that we break is a communion with the body of Christ. Because there is only one loaf means that we, though many, are one body because we all share the one loaf and the one cup.

(1) Love is always patient and kind, it is never jealous. Love is never boastful or conceited, it is never rude or selfish. Love takes no pleasure in other people's sins but delights in the truth. It is always ready to excuse, to trust, to hope and to endure whatever comes.

(2) Are you people in Galatia mad? Are you going to surrender the power of the Spirit and become slaves again? Surely you realise that Christ died for you and that you are now free?

(1) We are only earthenware jars that hold this treasure, to make it clear that such an overwhelming power comes from God and not from us. We are in difficulties on all sides but never fear; we see no answer to our problems but never despair.

(2) I thank my God each time I think of you and every time I pray for you, I pray with joy.

To help those assembled to reflect on their sinfulness the following text might be used.

Voice 1: Bless me Father for I have sinned; it is three weeks since my last confession.

Voice 2: It might be a month, a year, ten years, but we all need to speak about our real problems, our fears, our real failures.

There is nothing worse in life than carrying great burdens for years. We need to be released, to be healed, to be forgiven.

Voice 1: I cursed.

Voice 2: Yes I use some bad language but that is not cursing in the true sense. To curse is the opposite of to praise. We should give praise and thanks at all times; praise God for the wonder of creation; thank God and our forebears for the gift of life; dance for joy before the rainbow, the sea, the sky and the stars. But instead I find myself cursing my luck and I forget to give praise and thanks.

Voice 1: I stole.

Voice 2: I've never really stolen anything significant, or have I? I suppose that I've often stolen the wonder from people's lives by my moodiness. I've stolen other's dignity by refusing to acknowledge their value, their independence. I've stolen my own beauty by not treasuring the gift of my own life.

Voice 1: I didn't say my prayers.

Voice 2: Usually I just forget them. I remember to pray when I need something or I am stuck in a rut. Now that I have some time to think I should reflect about things. I have family and friends. My table is bountiful and my home warm. I can see the sunrise and the sunset and I can hear the wind and the rain. I am alive. However in my ordinary life I forget these things. To pray is to truly remember.

Voice 1: I lied.

Voice 2: We all tell the odd white lie. Yet it's easy to get into the habit of lying. I lie when I fail to see the truth in another person. The truth is that everyone is precious in God's eyes. Do I ever ask myself whether what I've heard is true or not? To speak the truth is difficult and demanding.

Voice 1: I missed Mass.

Voice 2: I know I should go because it's an obligation. But it can be very tedious and repetitive and I am easily distracted. Yet I am part of the great story that is being told. When the bread is broken so too I experience brokenness and difficulty. When the wine is poured so too am I asked to give of myself to the rest of the world. When the community gathered I wasn't present. I missed Mass and I missed out on part of who I am.

It is the common experience of Christians that they sin again after celebrating sacramental reconciliation. In order to strengthen them for the journey that lies ahead the following text might be read. Two readers are needed, one reads the spirit of the world and the other the spirit of God. In each case the spirit of the world comes first followed within a couple of seconds by the spirit of God; there is then a substantial pause (10-15 seconds) before moving on. The two readers should stand at the two lecterns.

(1) The spirit of the world says that externals are all important - looks, property, possessions. You are what you have.
(2) The spirit of God says that your looks and appearance can be very deceptive. You must look into the heart, into the depth of life to see who we really are.

(1) The spirit of the world says that life is a test and success is everything. It abhors failure and disappointment.
(2) The spirit of God says that failure can be more important than success. We can learn much even from the sad and more difficult times.

(1) The spirit of the world says that the great problems - unemployment, ecology, violence - have nothing to do with me. I've just got to mind my own patch.
(2) The spirit of God says that I am responsible for everyone, everywhere, at all times. There are no strangers in God's eyes.

(1) The spirit of the world says that love is about things going well, in accord with my plans.

(2) The spirit of God says that love is about giving of myself, even when I feel that I cannot.

(1) The spirit of the world says that there is no such thing as forgiveness because there is no such thing as sin.

(2) The spirit of God says that forgiveness is the greatest reality that we know. We sin, we fail, yet we can be freed to go on.

(1) The spirit of the world says that honesty and commitment are impossible and don't really exist.

(2) The spirit of God says that honesty and commitment are the only things that really matter in the end.

(1) The spirit of the world says that the sick and the disabled are not really alive. Sickness and disability are disastrous.

(2) The spirit of God says that the sick and the disabled are often those who are most alive for they know their dependence; they know that life is not in their control.

(1) The spirit of the world says that death is the end of life and proves that life is futile.

(2) The spirit of God says that death is not the end of life as the great spirit present in us is not extinguished but transformed.

Leader: Since all of us are members of the baptised community we will be anointed with chrism as a reminder of our baptism and confirmation. We received the Spirit of God in those sacraments and this oil reminds us that we must continue to struggle to give that Spirit free reign in our lives.

All present should be anointed with oil while the minister says:

God's Spirit has been poured into our hearts. May you be strengthened to live in accord with the values of God's Spirit.

The service might conclude with these or similar words:

You are the salt of the earth,
you are the light of the world,
together we are the body of Christ.
As a baby you were baptised in Christ,
at seven years you were invited to eat from the altar of
God,
and later the church confirmed the gift of God's Spirit
given to you.
Go now from this holy place,
treasure in your heart the wonder of who you are
and may the words you have heard here ever echo in your
mind.
You are the salt of the earth,
you are the light of the world,
together we are the body of Christ.

3. A Service of Healing

This ritual could include the formal anointing of the sick. Suitable music or songs can easily be woven into this service.

Leader: We are gathered as God's people in need of healing. Let us listen to God's word.

In each case a personal reflection comes first followed after a pause by a biblical quotation; there is then a further pause before moving on.

(1) We are children of the earth, made of the same stuff as the stars, we are part of the beauty of the earth.

(2) In the beginning God created the heavens and the earth. Now the earth was a formless void, there was darkness over the deep and God's Spirit hovered over the water. God saw what God had made and it was very good.

(1) Think of the date you were born, the joy of your parents, family, neighbours and friends. Imagine yourself as a baby.

(2) Before I formed you in the womb I knew you, before you came to birth I consecrated you.

(1) Recall in your own mind the various places you've lived. Think of the houses, the places - go into each of them in your mind.

(2) Wherever you go, I will go, wherever you live I will live.

(1) Think of a couple of really happy moments in your life. Treasure them in your heart.

(2) I want you to be happy, always happy in the Lord; I repeat, what I want is your happiness.

(1) Allow moments of suffering and pain to enter your mind. They are part of who we are.

(2) Come to me all you who labour and are overburdened and I will give you rest. For my yoke is easy and my burden is light.

(1) Who are the people who accompany you? - family, spouse, children, neighbours, friends? Look at their faces now.

(2) Did not our hearts burn within us as he talked to us on the road and explained the scriptures to us............ and their eyes were opened and they recognised him in the breaking of the bread.

(1) What do you hope for? What are your greatest expectations, your cherished dream?

(2) What we suffer in this life can never be compared to the glory which is yet to be revealed.

(1) Where will it all end? What will happen in the future?

(2) I saw a new heaven and a new earth...... Then I heard a loud voice call from above: now I am making the whole of creation new.

Leader: We are a eucharistic people on our way to God's kingdom. But on this journey we need support and healing.

Reader:

In the Eucharist bread is taken, blessed, broken and given. In life we are taken, blessed, broken and given.

The priest takes the bread in his hands and blesses it during the eucharistic prayer;

then he breaks it and it is given to us as the body of Christ. Through our birth and baptism we are taken into God's hands;

as the bread is taken, so too are we.

In life we are blessed by family, friends, love and joy;

as the bread is blessed, so too are we.

We are broken by failure, sin, pain and heartbreak;

as the bread is broken, so too are we.

In death we are given back to the mystery from which we came;

as the bread is given, so too are we.

When we take, bless, break and give bread to one another,
we believe the Lord to be especially present in our midst.
But we must learn to accept that in his memory
we will be taken, blessed, broken and given
for the life of the world.

If there is only a small number of people present the leader should invite them all to place one hand on the shoulder of each person while a member of the group says:

You are not afraid of dying to the old,
You are not afraid of giving birth to what is new,
You are not afraid of planting,
You are not afraid of uprooting what has been planted,
You are not afraid of searching,
You are not afraid of keeping or throwing away,
You are not afraid of tears or mourning,
You are not afraid of laughter.

If there is a large number of people present a priest should lay hands on each individual while saying:
May you receive healing and strength to face life's difficulties.

Once the participants are seated again the following reflection is read.

Lord God help me to let go.
Life is an endless process of letting go;
In our birth we had to let go of the security of our mother's womb and emerge into a strange world;
In adolescence we let go of the innocence of childhood;
All of us have to let go of home, parents must let go of their children and children must let go of their parents;
Throughout life as we grow and mature we must continually let go of opinions, jobs, good health and ultimately of the idea that we are in control.
And, of course, in death we must let go of those we love.

Between womb and tomb life is an endless process of letting go.

Come, Holy Spirit, help me to let go so that even when the letting go is tearful and sad it will awaken me to the mystery and wonder of life.

Life is the greatest gift we have received and in the end we must let go of this gift.

We must let go of the past to let God be the God of the future.

The community should often be reminded of the links between baptism, eucharist and healing. During services like these is a good time to renew baptismal promises. The text on pp. 144-5 could be used.

The service should close with a blessing.

4. Marriage

Given the nature of the sacrament of marriage the couple should be encouraged to plan the ceremony in some detail. Everything possible should be done to highlight the significance of the mutual giving of consent. The statement form should be used and ideally the couple should face the congregation. It should also be made clear to those involved that they do not have to follow particular traditions which are not part of the marriage rite. Thus the bride and groom might walk in a procession together which might also include some relatives. The law demands that there be two witnesses; there can be other bridesmaids and groomsmen but they are not formally witnesses of the marriage.

The couple could also compose some introductory words and reflections for use during the ceremony.

Introduction

One of the witnesses might introduce the ceremony as follows:

N and N you are here today in this sacred place to exchange the vows of your love for each other. We are here as your family and friends to support you as you wed. In the presence of God we will witness the promise of your love.

Candles

Sometimes it is customary for the bride and bridegroom to light two candles before the rite of marriage. Afterwards a flame is taken from each of these candles and a single candle is lit as a sign of the unity of marriage. Alternatively the parents of the bride and bridegroom can be asked to light these two candles with this text:

It was from our marriage that we gave you life. May you both give birth to another generation and may you be blessed with hope and happiness.

When the couple light the single candle they could use this text:
We thank God for the gift of life and the gift of love.

Giving of consent
The amount of time that it takes to exchange marital vows is very short. In order to give people time to reflect on the significance of what is happening, there should be some music or song or a spoken reflection after the giving of consent. These words might be spoken:

May you know joy in each other's company
And may your love carry you through the years ahead.

May your friends be plentiful and your table bountiful
And may God's face smile upon your home.

May laughter and pleasure be with you always
And may you grow old in the warmth of your embrace.

May compassion and understanding accompany you
And through forgiveness may your love turn to gold.

If the exchange of rings and other tokens takes place this should be mutual.

Prayer of thanksgiving
The couple should be encouraged to compose their own prayer. Here is an example:

We give thanks for our parents
And for the gift of life;
For their sacrifice,
Protection and a thousand hugs.

We give thanks for our family,
For fights and forgiveness,
For memories, too many to mention
And presents at Christmastime.

We give thanks for our friends,
For generosity and loyalty,
For laughter and sorrow,
And secrets kept.

We give thanks to God
for the waters of baptism;
For Jesus' self-sacrifice
and the Spirit of love.

In thanksgiving, we pray that we may be
As generous and as kind as you are.
And may our marriage strengthen us all the days of our life
To be truly Christian in faith, hope and love.

5. Death of an Infant

The most difficult pastoral situation of all is the death of an infant. The official rites of the church are very helpful at this time. Here we suggest some texts and symbols that might be of some benefit. Symbols are very important at times such as these when our words begin to flounder. The priest or other minister should encourage some of those present to read some of the texts.

Candles

Leader: After Jesus had died, the disciples hid in the upper room. Like us, they were filled with doubt and despair in the face of untimely death. They huddled together murmuring their confusion and whispering their loss. It was to such a group that God sent the Spirit at Pentecost to comfort their sorrow and sow understanding amidst confusion. The Spirit came in tongues of fire and as these candles are lit we ask God to send his Spirit to those who mourn today. These candles will be given to N and N (parents). May they be filled with the Spirit and believe that N, who died in Christ, will live forever.

The candles can be blessed and then lit. If appropriate those gathered can be invited to take a candle home with them.

Water

Reader: Before N was born he/she was nurtured and sustained in the womb. We celebrate a short life lived in the waters of warmth and comfort. It was a life free from sorrow or pain, cradled only in love and joyful expectation. Like our love for N, Christ's love for us is never ending.

For a baptised infant:

In his/her baptism N was reborn into the gift of everlasting life. N was born into our embrace and our love and now he/she has been reborn into the arms of God's love.

For an infant who died before baptism:

N was born into our embrace and our love and now, through death, he/she is reborn into the mystery of the love and mercy of God.

The priest then invites everyone present to bless themselves with water saying:

We have been baptised into the mystery of everlasting life. *Those gathered can be invited to take some of the blessed water home with them.*

Clothes

Reader: N, we held out for you the promise of life, yet unexpectedly this gift has been taken away from us all. We had arrangements made for you and a place prepared in our home. We had clothes to keep you warm, toys to keep you happy and a treasure of unspoken hopes and wishes. We wanted so much to care for you and prove our love. And so we wrap you in these cloths to keep you on your journey.

At this point the parents can wrap the infant in the cloths prepared saying:

May you find the care we had prepared for you with all the saints in heaven.

If the parents find it comforting and an expression of their care items may be placed in the coffin. The prayers of the faithful could accompany these.

The Lord's Prayer and the sign of peace

Leader: In these terrible hours we have wrung our hands in anguish and our eyes have been washed with tears of sorrow. Within this death there is an emptiness difficult to fathom and a silence which baffles our sense. It is with a weak voice that we cry to God and ask for the spirit of strength and acceptance.

All: The Lord's Prayer

The priest then blesses all present:

'Come to me, all you who labour and are overburdened, and I will give you rest.'

The rite could conclude with the sign of peace.

Parents and others bereaved should be encouraged to write about their thoughts and feelings. Such reflections might be used on occasions such as anniversaries. Here is one example:

A mother's prayer on the death of her child
The land of our promise was populated with every kind of hope for you,
Every kind of wish for your life.
We had imagined who you would be like;
Handsome and witty thought your father,
Practical and purposeful like your mother I claimed.
Little child why did you go away
Before you had learned to live at all?

They said you'd keep us up all night
That things would never be the same again.
Friends hoped to see your father with a nappy in his hand
With tired eyes and a sleepy head.
The fun we'd have putting you to bed.
Little child you have turned our world upside down
Our tired eyes and our sleepy heads.

Your father enthused about the talents on his side of the family
You'd be a professional, a doctor most likely!
I wondered what your ways would be like
Would you be grumpy like your grandfather
Or mellow and secretive like grandma?
The questions and questions that go round in my mind

You are a mystery and a feast of answers
An unknown martyr, and an innocent victim
Of the dark and terrible ways of this world.
One day this veil of mourning will be lifted
And we will be with you where you are now going.
Be there N to put your arms round us
For in you little child, we have seen a glimpse of heaven.

At the graveside
Reading: The empty tomb. John 20:1-10

Leader: We would not have chosen to gather here today beside this empty grave and at times like this we are forced to ponder the mysteries of life and death in Christ. The reading we have listened to tells us of the meaning of an empty grave. We look at this stark and lonely scene and our hearts, though like lead, are filled only with emptiness. In the story of the empty tomb, the other disciple, like us, did not want to look into an empty grave, afraid that he might only see death and hopelessness. But Peter went into the tomb and discovered not death but new life in the linen cloths gathered on the ground. N has gone into the tomb and died with Christ, but let these cloths that he/she was wrapped in be given to you as a sign of his/her new life in Christ.

It is suggested that a special cloth that the infant was wrapped in be then given to the parents saying:
Treasure this sacred cloth. N is alive in Christ.

Comforting signs regarding death and new life can be revealed in the rhythms of sowing and planting. It can be suggested to the parents that they plant a small garden on the grave with bulbs that will flower in springtime.

6. Funerals

Funeral practices vary from one culture to another. The Christian dimension of such rituals should emphasise the link with baptism. The following texts and symbols could be used in vigils for the deceased at home or in hospital or during the reception of the bodily remains in a church. Such vigils do not necessarily need the involvement of an ordained minister.

Leader:

It is in baptism that we enter eternal life. It is God's gift to us through water and the Holy Spirit that we are reborn into everlasting life. Let us think again about the meaning of our baptism.

The Paschal Candle
Attention can be drawn to the Paschal candle.

When God created the world there was darkness over the deep and God's Spirit hovered over the chaos. God said, 'Let there be light' and there was light. God saw that the light was good. The early Christians spoke of Jesus as the light that had come into the world and so they gathered in the evening darkness to commemorate his life. And then they lit a candle to celebrate his presence amongst them. *(Pause)*

When N was baptised he/she received the light of Christ. N was asked to keep the flame of faith alive until the Lord comes. Then he/she would meet him with all the saints of the heavenly kingdom.

Water
A jug and bowl of water can be used to focus on the blessed water.

Christ says: Let everyone who listens answer, 'Come'. Then let all who are thirsty come: all who want it may have the water of life, and have it free. As the Jews of old were led to new life through the waters of the Red Sea may

N be led from us to the water of new life.
(Pause)
N was brought to the waters of baptism as an infant. May all who are buried with Christ in the death of baptism also rise with him to newness of life.

Oil

A small bowl of oil can be used here.

One of the great gifts of God's creation is fruit-bearing trees. From the fruit of the olive tree oil is pressed. In the Old Testament, people were anointed with oil to make them sacred. Of old the Jews spoke of David as God's anointed, the one set apart to be their king. The early Christians spoke of Jesus as the new David and so they called him Christ which means 'the anointed one'.
(Pause)
In baptism N was anointed with the chrism of salvation and welcomed into God's holy people. Just as Christ was anointed Priest, Prophet and King, N was born into Christ's body in order to share in the wonder of everlasting life. May the oils of our baptism strengthen us today in the face of sorrow and loss.

The following text might be read. Two readers are required.

(1) Our hearts are heavy at the loss of N.

(2) Come to me all you who labour and are overburdened, and I will give you rest. Shoulder my yoke and learn from me, for I am gentle and humble in heart and you will find rest for your souls. Yes, my yoke is easy and my burden light.

(1) Naturally we ask at this time, why do people die?

(2) Unless a wheat grain falls on the ground and dies, it remains only a single grain; but if it dies it yields a rich harvest.

(1) It is hard to believe that N who has died will live forever.

(2) I am the resurrection. If anyone believes in me, even though he dies he will live, and whoever lives and believes in me will never die.

(1) We pray today in hope that N who has died is at peace.

(2) Only in God is my soul at rest, from him comes my hope. He alone is my rock, my fortress. Unburden your hearts onto him for God is our shelter.

(1) It is difficult to understand why our family and friends must die.

(2) St Paul says that God's foolishness is wiser than human wisdom and God's weakness is stronger than human strength. It is when I am weak that I am strong, for I feel the power of Christ shining through my human weakness.

(1) We do not know what the future holds for those who have died but we trust in God's promise.

(2) May the choirs of angels welcome you and lead you to Abraham's side. Where Lazarus is poor no longer, may you have eternal rest.

Texts for use in rituals

1. Letting go

This text should simply be read reflectively by one reader.

Lord God help me to let go.

Life is an endless process of letting go;

In our birth we had to let go of the security of our mother's womb and emerge into a strange world;

In adolescence we let go of the innocence of childhood;

All of us have to let go of home, parents must let go of their children and children must let go of their parents;

Throughout life as we grow and mature we must continually let go of opinions, jobs, good health and ultimately of the idea that we are in control.

And, of course, in death we must let go of those we love.

Between womb and tomb life is an endless process of letting go.

Come, Holy Spirit, help me to let go so that even when the letting go is tearful and sad it will awaken me to the mystery and wonder of life.

Life is the greatest gift we have received and we must in the end let go of this gift.

We must let go of the past to let God be the God of the future.

2. Fear

Each line begins with 'I am', 'you are' or 'we are'. This text is particularly suitable when read along with Ecclesiastes 3:1-8.

For adults:

You are not afraid of dying to the old,
You are not afraid of giving birth to what is new,
You are not afraid of planting,
You are not afraid of uprooting what has been planted,
You are not afraid of searching,
You are not afraid of keeping or throwing away,
You are not afraid of tears or mourning,
You are not afraid of laughter.

For adolescents:

You are not afraid of dying to childhood ways,
You are not afraid of giving birth to wisdom and courage,
You are not afraid of planting responsibility in your life,
You are not afraid of uprooting what needs to be changed,
You are not afraid of searching for the man/woman that is within you,
You are not afraid of becoming independent and free,
You are not afraid of mourning your break with the past,
You are not afraid of embracing the future.

3. I am

This text should simply be read reflectively by one reader.

I am the wind of the sea,
I am the wave of the ocean,
I am the wind that blows,
I am the fire that burns.

I am not afraid of dying,
I am not afraid of searching,
I have gone where I would rather not go,
I have drunk from the water of life.

4. The power of Paul's words

There should be two readers reciting the texts alternatively with a short pause between each one. Ideally the two readers should stand at lecterns at opposite ends of the relevant space.

1   The word of God cuts more finely than a double-edged sword. It cuts between the marrow and the bone so that the truth can emerge.

2   What we preach is Christ crucified; a scandal for Jews and folly for Greeks, but for us, who believe, the wisdom and the glory of God. For God's foolishness is wiser than human wisdom, and God's weakness is stronger than human strength.

1   It is when I am weak that I am strong, for I feel the power of Christ shining through my human weakness.

2   I, Paul, appointed by God to be an apostle, send greetings to the church of God in Corinth, to the holy people of Jesus Christ who are called to take their place among all the saints everywhere. May God our Father and the Lord Jesus Christ send you grace and peace.

1   Nothing can ever come between us and the love of God made visible in Christ Jesus our Lord. No angel, no power, no division, no fear can ever separate us from the love of God.

2   The blessing cup that we bless is a communion with the blood of Christ and the bread that we break is a communion with the body of Christ. Because there is only one loaf means that we, though many, are one body because we all share the one loaf and the one cup.

1   Love is always patient and kind, it is never jealous. Love is never boastful or conceited, it is never rude or selfish. Love takes no pleasure in other people's sins but delights in the truth. It is always ready to excuse, to trust, to hope and to endure whatever comes.

2   Are you people in Galatia mad? Are you going to surrender
    the power of the Spirit and become slaves again?   Surely
    you realise that Christ died for you and that you are now
    free?

1   We are only earthenware jars that hold this treasure, to
    make it clear that such an overwhelming power comes
    from God and not from us. We are in difficulties on all
    sides but never fear; we see no answer to our problems but
    never despair.

2   I thank my God each time I think of you and every time I
    pray for you, I pray with joy.

5. The spirit of God and the spirit of the world

Two readers are needed, one reads the spirit of the world and the other the spirit of God. In each case the spirit of the world comes first followed within a couple of seconds by the spirit of God; there is then a substantial pause (10-15 seconds) before moving on. Ideally the two readers should stand at lecterns at opposite ends of the relevant space.

1   The spirit of the world says that externals are all important – looks, property, possessions. You are what you have.

2   The spirit of God says that your looks and appearance can be very deceptive. You must look into the heart, into the depth of life to see who we really are.

1   The spirit of the world says that life is a test and success is everything. It abhors failure and disappointment.

2   The spirit of God says that failure can be more important than success. We can learn much even from the sad and more difficult times.

1   The spirit of the world says that the great problems – unemployment, ecology, violence – have nothing to do with me. I've just got to mind my own patch.

2   The spirit of God says that I am responsible for everyone, everywhere, at all times. There are no strangers in God's eyes.

1   The spirit of the world says that love is about things going well, in accord with my plans.

2   The spirit of God says that love is about giving of myself, even when I feel that I cannot.

1   The spirit of the world says that there is no such thing as forgiveness because there is no such thing as sin.

2   The spirit of God says that forgiveness is the greatest reality that we know. We sin, we fail, yet we can be freed to go on.

1   The spirit of the world says that honesty and commitment are impossible and don't really exist.

2   The spirit of God says that honesty and commitment are
    the only things that really matter in the end.

1   The spirit of the world says that the sick and the disabled
    are not really alive. Sickness and disability are disastrous.

2   The spirit of God says that the sick and the disabled are
    often those who are most alive for they know their depen-
    dence; they know that life is not in their control.

1   The spirit of the world says that death is the end of life and
    proves that life is futile.

2   The spirit of God says that death is not the end of life as
    the great spirit present in us is not extinguished but trans-
    formed.

6. The community of Pentecost

This text can be read by one or more readers.

Remember the famous scene in the upper room when the disciples and Mary were waiting for the gift of the Spirit. Did you ever think much about the reality that they faced? In many ways that group, which included Mary the Mother of Jesus, was very akin to our gathering here today.

Some people in the upper room were doubtful about what it was all about; similarly some of us here are doubtful, wondering if we should be here at all.

Some were enthusiastic, bursting to tell the message to others; undoubtedly some of us are enthusiastic to get out there and tell people the good news.

Some of the disciples were very confused by everything that had happened to them; some of us are very confused by what has happened to us in our lives.

Some of the folk had grown cynical about the whole thing, believing that they had been fooled; maybe some of us have grown cynical too, having seen so much that disheartens us in the church and in religion in general.

Some of the disciples were broken by all the suffering and death they had witnessed; some of us are broken by life, by illness, by death.

Others of the disciples were worried and didn't know where to turn; some of us carry great worries about what the future holds.

Presumably some of the people in the upper room were bored, wondering if anything was ever going to happen; some of us probably find life tedious and wonder if it has any value.

And finally there were those who were deeply hopeful in the midst of it all, trusting in God's promise; equally there are people of deep hope and joy sitting in our midst today.

So if you count yourself somewhere, anywhere, amongst those who are doubtful, enthusiastic, confused, cynical, broken, worried, bored, hopeful or joyful, then take great heart for it was to such as these that the Spirit of God was first given. It was to a motley crew like ourselves that God gave the greatest gift: not to those who had all the answers, nor to those who had life all sewn up, but rather to those who were struggling with the realities of life.

Note: instead of saying 'some of us' or 'some people' in the second phrase, one could say – 'all of us at times are …'.

7. My story with biblical eyes

In each case a personal reflection comes first followed after a pause by a biblical quotation; there is then a further pause before moving on. Ideally the two readers should stand at lecterns at opposite ends of the relevant space.

1 We are children of the earth, made of the same stuff as the stars; we are part of the beauty of the earth.

2 In the beginning God created the heavens and the earth. Now the earth was a formless void, there was darkness over the deep and God's Spirit hovered over the water. God saw what God had made and it was very good.

1 Think of the date you were born, the joy of your parents, family, neighbours and friends. Imagine yourself as a baby.

2 Before I formed you in the womb I knew you, before you came to birth I consecrated you.

1 Recall in your own mind the various places you've lived. Think of the houses, the places – go into each of them in your mind.

2 Wherever you go, I will go, wherever you live I will live.

1 Think of a couple of really happy moments in your life. Treasure them in your heart.

2 I want you to be happy, always happy in the Lord; I repeat, what I want is your happiness.

1 Allow moments of suffering and pain to enter your mind. They are part of who we are.

2 Come to me all you who labour and are overburdened and I will give you rest. For my yoke is easy and my burden is light.

1 Who are the people who accompany you? – family, spouse, children, neighbours, friends? Look at their faces now.

2 Did not our hearts burn within us as he talked to us on the road and explained the scriptures to us … and their eyes were opened and they recognised him in the breaking of the bread.

1 What do you hope for? What are your greatest expectations, your cherished dream?
2 What we suffer in this life can never be compared to the glory which is yet to be revealed.
1 Where will it all end? What will happen in the future?
2 I saw a new heaven and a new earth … Then I heard a loud voice call from above: now I am making the whole of creation new.

8. A blessing on leaving a Christian gathering

This text should simply be read reflectively by one reader.

You are the salt of the earth,
you are the light of the world,
together we are the body of Christ.
As a baby you were baptised in Christ,
at seven years you were invited to eat from the altar of God,
and later the church confirmed the gift of God's Spirit given
to you.
Go now from this holy place,
treasure in your heart the wonder of who you are
and may the words you have heard here ever echo in your
mind.
You are the salt of the earth,
you are the light of the world,
together we are the body of Christ.

9. Take, bless, break and give

This text should simply be read reflectively by one reader.

In the Eucharist bread is taken, blessed, broken and given.
In life we are taken, blessed, broken and given.
The priest takes the bread in his hands and blesses it during
the eucharistic prayer;
then he breaks it and it is given to us as the body of Christ.
Through our birth and baptism we are taken into God's
hands;
as the bread is taken, so too are we.
In life we are blessed by family, friends, love and joy;
as the bread is blessed, so too are we.
We are broken by failure, sin, pain and heartbreak;
as the bread is broken, so too are we.
In death we are given back to the mystery from which we
came;
as the bread is given, so too are we.
When we take, bless, break and give bread to one another,
we believe the Lord to be especially present in our midst.
But we must learn to accept that in his memory
we will be taken, blessed, broken and given
for the life of the world.

10. Renewal of baptismal promises

Leader: Do you believe in God the creator of light and darkness, land and sea, heaven and earth, woman and man?

All: We do.

Leader: Do you cherish and protect the earth as God's creation?

All: We do.

Leader: Do you appreciate the gift of water which endlessly renews and sustains life?

All: We do.

Leader: Do you give thanks for the spring and the summer, the sowing and the harvest, the sun and the moon, the wind and the rain, the mountain top and the sea shore?

All: We do.

Leader: Do you believe that in the midst of a beautiful world we, like Adam and Eve, live in the shadow of temptation and evil?

All: We do.

Leader: Do you reject all that is evil?

All: We do.

Leader: Do you reject injustice, hatred, despair and bigotry?

All: We do.

Leader: Do you reject all that undermines and destroys the gift of life?

All: We do.

Leader: Do you believe that Jesus Christ is the Saviour of the world?

All: We do.

Leader: Do you believe that Jesus died for us on Calvary and was raised from the dead?

All: We do.

Leader: Do you believe that in baptism you became followers of Jesus?

All: We do.

Leader: Do you believe that when you were anointed with oil in baptism you received the gift of God's Spirit?

All: We do.

Leader: Do you believe that God's Spirit is present in humanity and that our destiny is to share fully in God's own life?

All: We do.

Leader: Do you accept the Christian identity that was given to you in your name at baptism?

All: We do.

Leader: Do you accept that your faith can only be lived with others in a Christian community?

All: We do.

Leader: Do you believe that the church, a community of saints and sinners, is the temple of God's presence in the world?

All: We do.

Leader: Do you take responsibility for the future well-being of the church?

All: We do.

Leader: Do you believe in the final triumph of Christ over sin, light over darkness, truth over lies, hope over despair, good over evil and life over death?

All: We do.

Leader: Do you today, in the presence of fellow believers, confirm the meaning and implications of your baptism?

All: We do.

Leader: Do you now promise to live your life in accordance with the Christian faith which we have professed together?

All: We do.

Leader: Then may God bless you and strengthen you as you bear witness to your faith.

11. Peter's faith (according to John's Gospel)

Three readers are required. This text can simply be read reflectively or acted out as a role play.

Voice 1: In the evening of the first day of the week, Jesus showed himself to his disciples. He turned to Simon Peter and said: 'Simon, son of John, do you love me?'

Voice 2: Yes Lord, you know I love you.

Voice 3: While Simon Peter and another disciple were standing outside the door of the high priest's house, the woman keeping the door said to him – 'aren't you one of that man's disciples?'

Voice 2: I am not.

Voice 1: Jesus asked again: 'Simon, son of John, do you love me?'

Voice 2: Yes Lord, you know I love you.

Voice 3: One of the servants turned to Peter and said: 'You are one of his disciples surely; didn't I see you with him?'

Voice 2: I tell you I do not know the man.

Voice 1: A third time Jesus said: 'Simon, son of John, do you love me?'

Voice 2: Yes Lord, you know all things, you know I love you.

Voice 3: A woman standing by the fire turned to Peter and said: 'You are one of his disciples. Why, you are a Galilean! Your accent gives you away.'

Voice 2: I tell you I don't know what you are talking about. I swear I never saw the man.

Voice 1: You are Peter and upon this rock I will build my church. Feed my lambs. Feed my sheep.

12. Affirming the Christian commitment of women

Two readers are required.

First voice: Ruth's mother-in-law was called Naomi and she had lost both her sons. In desperation and loneliness she decided to return to her homeland. She told Ruth that she had no more sons and that life with her had no future. However Ruth did not desert her mother-in-law. She said to her: 'Wherever you go I will go, wherever you live I will live.'

Pause

May you like Ruth be blessed with faithfulness and perseverance. As pilgrims on the journey of life, may you remain steadfast in your faith even in the midst of disillusionment and disappointment.

Second voice: After the resurrection, and whilst the followers of Jesus cowered in despair and fear, Mary of Magdala set out to tend the body of Jesus. Through this act of courage she became the first person to encounter the risen Christ. Jesus then sent this woman to bring the good news to the others.

Pause

As women in the church, may you show leadership in the face of doubt and dejection. Continue to believe in the promises of Christ so that you may be a wellspring of healing and hope in a broken world.

First voice: Mary as a young mother said 'yes' to the will of God. She nurtured the divine in the human and in her womb bore God to the world. Mary followed her son all the way to the cross.

Pause

As women in the church, say 'yes' to God's word and nurture the divine presence in the human. As mothers, build a church that is home to all.

13. Affirming the Christian commitment of men

Two readers are required.

First voice: As a young man Jeremiah was told by God 'before I formed you in the womb I knew you, before you came to birth I consecrated you'. Jeremiah was consecrated as a prophet and became a man who courageously spoke the truth. Many did not want to hear what he said because he condemned the wrongdoer and gave hope to the outcast.

Pause

Second voice: As men, the world tells you to be powerful, to accumulate wealth and popularity. It tells you to be successful, to do well for yourself. May you be blessed like Jeremiah as prophet and speaker of the truth. Tell the world that the voice of the Spirit says be charitable, be merciful, forgive those who wrong you, and be honest and just in your dealings always.

First voice: When the Hebrews were slaves in Egypt they cried out to God to free them. God called Moses to liberate his people. He used no weapons, had no army, yet the spirit of the warrior within him fought and challenged the powers that held the people in bondage. God blessed the courage of this man and empowered him to lead the Hebrews through the waters of the Red Sea and into freedom.

Pause

Second voice: As men, may God bless you with a brave heart to fight for the liberation of men and women from the oppression of injustice and despair.

First voice: John the Baptist wore a garment of camel skin and he lived on locusts and wild honey. His home was the wilderness and his work was to preach repentance and to baptise in the waters of the Jordan. He was an outcast and lived alone, yet this man prepared the way for the Lord. It was this wild man that announced the coming of Christ into the world.

Pause

As men, may you find within yourselves the energy and
courage to speak about Christ and prepare a way for his
message in your homes, your places of work and in your
communities.

14. Affirming the Christian commitment of the ordained

Two readers are required.

First voice: The name Abraham means Great Father. He was a
  man who had to leave his family, his father's house and his
  country to go to the land that God had shown him. He
  was to become the greatest of pilgrims. God blessed him
  and made of him a great nation.

Pause

Second voice: As a priest, you too have sacrificed the comforts
  of home in order to lead your people as pilgrims on a
  spiritual journey. May God bless you and your work.

First voice: Solomon was consecrated king of his people. God
  offered him any gift that he wanted. He asked for a heart
  to govern his people and to know right from wrong.

Pause

Second voice: We pray that like Solomon, people will say of you:
  You give justice to the poor,
  You save children from poverty,
  You free the lowly and helpless who call on you,
  You take pity on the poor and weak,
  And the souls of the powerless you save
  For they are precious in your eyes. *(see Psalm 72:4, 12-14)*

First voice: Paul who once zealously persecuted Christians was
  filled with the spirit of God to courageously preach Christ
  crucified. In the infancy of the church he formed communities of service and provided leadership to those who were
  lost and downhearted.

Pause

Second voice: As priests, do all you can to preserve the unity of
  your communities. Bring reconciliation where there is division, comfort where there is loss, and hope where there is
  despair. And glory be to God whose power working in you
  can do infinitely more than you can ask or even imagine.

15. Examination of Conscience

Two readers are required.

Voice 1: Bless me Father for I have sinned; it is three weeks since my last confession.

Voice 2: It might be a month, a year, ten years, but we all need to speak about our real problems, our fears, our real failures. There is nothing worse in life than carrying great burdens for years. We need to be released, to be healed, to be forgiven.

Voice 1: I cursed.

Voice 2: Yes, I use some bad language but that is not cursing in the true sense. To curse is the opposite of to praise. We should give praise and thanks at all times; praise God for the wonder of creation; thank God and our forebears for the gift of life; dance for joy before the rainbow, the sea, the sky and the stars. But instead I find myself cursing my luck and I forget to give praise and thanks.

Voice 1: I stole.

Voice 2: I've never really stolen anything significant, or have I? I suppose that I've often stolen the wonder from people's lives by my moodiness. I've stolen others' dignity by refusing to acknowledge their value, their independence. I've stolen my own beauty by not treasuring the gift of my own life.

Voice 1: I didn't say my prayers.

Voice 2: Usually I just forget them. I remember to pray when I need something or I am stuck in a rut. Now that I have some time to think, I should reflect about things. I have family and friends. My table is bountiful and my home warm. I can see the sunrise and the sunset and I can hear the wind and the rain. I am alive. However, in my ordinary life I forget these things. To pray is to truly remember.

Voice 1: I lied.

Voice 2: We all tell the odd white lie. Yet it's easy to get into the habit of lying. I lie when I fail to see the truth in another person. The truth is that everyone is precious in God's eyes. Do I ever ask myself whether what I've heard is true or not? To only speak the truth is difficult and demanding.

Voice 1: I missed Mass.

Voice 2: I know I should go because it's an obligation. But it can be very tedious and repetitive and I am easily distracted. Yet I am part of the great story that is being told. When the bread is broken, so too I experience brokenness and difficulty. When the wine is poured, so too am I asked to give of myself to the rest of the world. When the community gathered I wasn't present. I missed Mass and I missed out on part of who I am.

16. A Blessing on Getting Married

This text should be read reflectively by one reader.

May you know joy in each other's company
And may your love carry you through the years ahead.

May your friends be plentiful and your table bountiful
And may God's face smile upon your home.

May laughter and pleasure be with you always
And may you grow old in the warmth of your embrace.

May compassion and understanding accompany you
And through forgiveness may your love turn to gold.

17. Prayer of a newly married couple

The couple could read this text together, or each person might read alternate verses.

We give thanks for our parents
And for the gift of life;
For their sacrifice,
Protection and a thousand hugs.

We give thanks for our family,
For fights and forgiveness,
For memories, too many to mention
And presents at Christmastime.

We give thanks for our friends,
For generosity and loyalty,
For laughter and sorrow,
And secrets kept.

We give thanks to God
for the waters of baptism;
For Jesus' self-sacrifice
and the Spirit of love.

In thanksgiving, we pray that we may be
As generous and as kind as you are.
And may our marriage strengthen us all the days of our life
To be truly Christian in faith, hope and love.

18. A mother's prayer on the death of her child

The context will determine how best to use a text like this.

The land of our promise was populated with every kind of
hope for you,
Every kind of wish for your life.
We had imagined who you would be like;
Handsome and witty thought your father,
Practical and purposeful like your mother, I claimed.
Little child, why did you go away
Before you had learned to live at all?

They said you'd keep us up all night,
That things would never be the same again.
Friends hoped to see your father with a nappy in his hand,
With tired eyes and a sleepy head.
The fun we'd have putting you to bed.
Little child, you have turned our world upside down,
Our tired eyes and our sleepy heads.

Your father enthused about the talents on his side of the family.
You'd be a professional, a doctor most likely!
I wondered what your ways would be like;
Would you be grumpy like your grandfather,
Or mellow and secretive like grandma?
The questions and questions that go round in my mind.

You are a mystery and a feast of answers,
An unknown martyr, and an innocent victim
Of the dark and terrible ways of this world.
One day this veil of mourning will be lifted
And we will be with you where you are now going.
Be there, N, to put your arms round us,
For in you, little child, we have seen a glimpse of heaven.

19. Reflecting on death

Two readers are required.

(1) Our hearts are heavy at the loss of N.

(2) Come to me all you who labour and are overburdened, and I will you rest. Shoulder my yoke and learn from me, for I am gentle and humble in heart and you will find rest for your souls. Yes, my yoke is easy and my burden light.

(1) Naturally we ask at this time why do people die?

(2) Unless a wheat grain falls on the ground and dies, it remains only a single grain; but if it dies it yields a rich harvest.

(1) It is hard to believe that N who has died will live forever.

(2) I am the resurrection. If anyone believes in me, even though he dies he will live, and whoever lives and believes in me will never die.

(1) We pray today in hope that N, who has died, is at peace.

(2) Only in God is my soul at rest, from him comes my hope. He alone is my rock, my fortress. Unburden your hearts onto him for God is our shelter.

(1) It is difficult to understand why our family and friends must die.

(2) St Paul says that God's foolishness is wiser than human wisdom and God's weakness is stronger than human strength. It is when I am weak that I am strong, for I feel the power of Christ shining through my human weakness.

(1) We do not know what the future holds for those who have died but we trust in God's promise.

(2) May the choirs of angels welcome you and lead you to Abraham's side. Where Lazarus is poor no longer, may you have eternal rest.